W9-ANR-403

Filmmakers and Financing
Fourth Edition

Filmmakers and Financing
Fourth Edition

Business Plans
for Independents

Louise Levison

AMSTERDAM • BOSTON • HEIDELBERG • LONDON • NEW YORK • OXFORD
PARIS • SAN DIEGO • SAN FRANCISCO • SINGAPORE • SYDNEY • TOKYO

Focal Press is an imprint of Elsevier

Focal Press is an imprint of Elsevier
200 Wheeler Road, Burlington, MA 01803, USA
Linacre House, Jordan Hill, Oxford OX2 8DP, UK

Copyright © 2004, Louise Levison. All rights reserved.

No part of this publication may be reproduced, stored in a retrieval system,
or transmitted in any form or by any means, electronic, mechanical, photocopying,
recording, or otherwise, without the prior written permission of the publisher.

Permissions may be sought directly from Elsevier's Science & Technology Rights
Department in Oxford, UK: phone: (+44) 1865 843830, fax: (+44) 1865 853333,
e-mail: permissions@elsevier.com.uk. You may also complete your request
on-line via the Elsevier Science homepage (http://elsevier.com), by selecting
"Customer Support" and then "Obtaining Permissions."

 Recognizing the importance of preserving what has been written, Elsevier prints its
books on acid-free paper whenever possible.

Library of Congress Cataloging-in-Publication Data

Levison, Louise
    Filmmakers and financing : business plans for independents / Louise Levison.—
4th ed.
        p. cm.
    Includes index.
    ISBN 0–240–80536–4
        1. Motion pictures—Production and direction. 2. Motion picture industry—
Finance. I. Title.

PN1995.9.P7L433 2003
791.4302'32'0681—dc22   2003049509

British Library Cataloguing-in-Publication Data
A catalogue record for this book is available from the British Library.

ISBN: 0–240–80536–4

For information on all Focal Press publications
visit our website at www.focalpress.com

03 04 05 06 07 08 10 9 8 7 6 5 4 3 2 1

Printed in the United States of America

For Leonard the Wonder Cat who has left us but
continues to inspire…
And the new kids on the block, Buffy and Angel.

Contents

9

10

11

CD Table of Contents

Worksheets

Foreword

Despite the near hero-worship accorded successful independent film producers and studio executives, not one of them would be able to function without a strong backup team. The myth of the one-person band is just that—a myth. Without the talent and hard work of the lawyers, bankers, accountants, development personnel, and administrative staff—not to mention the literally hundreds of people involved in actually making the films—no independent producer could survive, much less succeed.

To marshal all the disparate talents involved in mounting a major film production, the most important element is a common vision of the ultimate end product. In the same way that directors need a storyboard to communicate their vision of what the film will look like, producers need their own version of a storyboard (that is, a business plan) to explain their objectives, hopes, aspirations, and, yes, even their dreams.

Gone are the days when a business plan was regarded as inappropriate for an artistic endeavor such as producing a film. These days, the risks are too large, the competition too intense, and the sophistication of investors too great to "leave the details until later." Completion guarantees, discounted cash flows, letters of credit, foreign sales contracts, domestic distribution deals, internal rates of return, gross deals, rolling breaks, third-party participants' security interest, bank discounting, residuals, cross-collateralization— all these terms, to name just a few, have become part of the regular vocabulary of today's independent producers. Without a detailed business plan to coordinate all these elements, it would be virtually impossible to produce a major film. So, dear independent producer, read on. . . .

Jake Eberts

Acknowledgments

To all the clients and students who have taught me as much as I have taught them

To all the industry professionals who have generously given of their time in classes and seminars to share their knowledge

To Jake Eberts for graciously contributing to this book

To David Russell for sharing his expertise on short film distribution

To Michael Donaldson, Bill Whitacre, Michael Norman Salesman, Robert Seigel, Rick Pamplin, Paul Sirmons, Karen Corrigan, Harlan Schneider, Dr. Linda Seger, and John Johnson whose comments on and contributions to the text are greatly appreciated

To Suzy Prudden and Terrel Miller for helping me keep my mind and body in balance after spending hours at the computer

To everyone at The Coffee Roaster for helping feed the mind as well as the body

To Bill, Helen, Jeffrey, and Carl for their support and understanding

To Rodney Gray for the many hours he spent critiquing the financial lessons on the CD

To Angela Agne for her checking the text

To Faryl Saliman Reingold for her editorial contributions and comments and her tireless efforts to keep me on track

To my editor Elinor Actipis and everyone else at Focal Press for their patience and understanding

And last, but not least, to the late Leonard the Wonder Cat for his personal inspiration for the cat tales

Introduction

Controlling Your Destiny

Independent doesn't have to be a synonym for badly made.
ROBERT REDFORD

WHY SHOULD YOU BUY THIS BOOK?

King Ferdinand of Spain appointed a group of consultants to advise him on Christopher Columbus's enterprise for sailing to the Indies. This scholarly group of astronomers, mariners, and pilots pored over charts and graphs. They determined not only that the world was flat, but also that the ocean was too big to be conquered.

"Ergo," they said, "if you try to sail to the Indies, you will fail." But Columbus had done his homework and planned ahead. He replied, "I have researched my own charts and graphs, spoken to other sailors, and obtained years of technical experience that proves otherwise. I believe it can be done." Columbus was the prototypical entrepreneur. He examined his proposed business venture, made forecasts regarding pros and cons and plunder versus expenses, and then he decided to move ahead.

Neither Columbus nor any of his friends or enemies knew that he would run into the Americas on his journey. Nevertheless, he seized his opportunity and took appropriate action. By keeping abreast of the situation on his ships, and the changes in the outside environment, he was able to make an informed decision. When he landed in the wrong place, Columbus looked at the opportunity, measured it against his goals, and decided that he had discovered a better place than he had originally intended.

From the dawn of film—actually, from the dawn of time—there have been individuals who have wanted to do it their own way. People who are not content to live by the rules of others continually strike out on their own. Here we are in 2003. The world is in turmoil with terrorists and strange viruses, governments are changing, corporations are failing, and the number of independent filmmakers keeps growing.

Tactics for a Constantly Changing Medium

My friend Jerry Quigg suggested calling this book *sex, films, and investing*. Good title. It is clear, informative, and to the point. All the elements for a book or a business plan are there. Your finest hour will come when an investor says, "What a sexy idea! It will make me money. How much do you want?" This book is sexy, too, in its own business-like way. It will bridge the gap for you between the passion of filmmaking and the day-to-day realities of creating a successful company.

As you read this, the motion picture business is changing right before your eyes. Studios have been shifting their focus a lot over the last six years, when Japanese manufacturers of hardware components were buying major studios, and cable and telephone companies were bidding for those that were left to control as much of the information superhighway as possible. Now the studios are looking for half or more of their productions funds to come from outside investors, Universal is in play again after only three years, and the cable/telephone conglomerates are fighting to stay alive.

Analysts have been predicting that the "paradigm" (a current in-vogue word meaning "pattern") of the motion picture business would change, but opinions differ as to when. It's happened. What hasn't changed is the audience. No matter what is happening in the world or the industry, they keep going to the movies.

All those hungry monoliths are looking more often to independents for their product. No matter how many products divide the finite viewing audience, theatrical motion pictures keep chugging down the track. Product is needed to fuel that engine, and you can be the one to provide it.

People go into independent filmmaking for many reasons. They are driven primarily by the subject matter, theme, or style of the pictures they want to make. I have talked to thousands of people who have told me what types of films they want to make.

No two people have had the same vision, but they all share one particular goal—to own their project and control it. Once a film-maker decides to make one film or many, it is up to him or her to understand how the business world functions. Of course, your goal may not be feature films at all. Instead, you may focus on other types of films, DVDs, television, or cable. All of these are important, and all the principles stated in this book apply equally to them.

With new opportunities appearing for the independent film-maker, more and more people want their own companies. Books and articles have been written about the ins and outs of writing or finding the perfect script, how much it costs to make a film, finding the best location, and what camera to use. None of that information is in this book. The question before us is not how to make a film, but how to get the money.

You might argue, "But I'm making *films*. This is different from other businesses." The details of business may differ from industry to industry and from segment to segment, but the principles are the same. Movies involve lots of people, all of whom expect to get paid. Raising money involves intermediaries such as agents, finders, and lawyers, who expect to get a fee for what they do—and do not forget the investor, who hopes to see a return on the investment. All companies need certain standard ingredients to get going and stay alive. To get the show on the road, you need to put together a business plan.

It is true that many firms have been launched and gone on to success without a business plan. Many more firms without one, however, have failed. Just read the newspaper or turn on the television. Owners start undercapitalized and go downhill from there. No plan can guarantee the thrill of victory, but not having a plan will bring you closer to the agony of defeat. When you read about all those production companies setting up shop with a large influx of capital from some foreign source, which of these scenarios do you believe?

1. SCENARIO 1: Louise, you've had such extraordinary success at Megalomaniac Studios that we would like to give you $100 million. Have fun and send us our share.
2. SCENARIO 2: Louise, you've had such extraordinary success at Megalomaniac Studios that we would like to explore the possibility of having you head your own

company with $100 million in seed capital. Why don't you get together with Victor Visionary from Major Merge Investment Group and create a business plan? If we agree with your product analysis and the numbers look good, we're in business.

Trust me (famous Hollywood term), Scenario 2 is far more likely. People do not throw around big bucks on a whim. The original idea—"Louise has a good idea; let's give her the money to make a film"—may be a whim. Before that impulse becomes a reality, however, much thinking and analysis will be done. Someone will ask for—you guessed it—a business plan.

The purpose of this book is to show you how to make all that thinking and analyzing into a coherent story. It is more than just an outline, however. The standard business plan outline has not changed for over 100 years. Open any book on business planning and you will see

- Summary
- Company
- Product
- Marketing
- Selling
- Financing

The question is not the formula, but what do you do next? This book will help you take the next step to expound and polish your business plan within those guidelines. It specifies not only what you need to include, but also why and how. I will give you samples—both good and bad—for writing the individual sections of your business plan. In the rest of this introduction, we will explore the reason for going through these exercises.

Movies as a Business

The biggest misconception about the movie business is that the *movie* is more important than the *business*. Many of us tend to think about filmmaking not as a business at all, but as an art form; in that case, it would be called *show art* instead of *show business*.

A movie *is* a form of art, but a very expensive one. Often the most difficult concept for filmmakers is looking at the movie as a commercial enterprise. The word *commercial* can be viewed in two very different ways. When it comes to artistic endeavors, many people give the word a negative connotation. The strict definition is "prepared for sale," but in many people's minds, the words "without regard to quality" are added to the end of that definition. Looking at it in the broader sense, however, the filmmaker trades a seat at the film for someone else's dollar (or $4, $9, or $15 as the case may be). Whether this trade occurs at a multiplex mall theater or at a video store, the buyer expects to get value for the trade, and value is definitely in the eye of the beholder.

When *Sling Blade* received an Academy Award nomination for Best Adapted Screenplay and another for Billy Bob Thornton for Best Actor and earned $50 million worldwide, one of the critics said that it was just another commercial, predictable film. Makes you wonder what films he's been watching, doesn't it? Even Billy Bob Thornton, the writer-director-actor, thought it would garner only a small audience. It combined several factors that blocked funds from production companies—a mentally defective ax-murderer for a lead character and a nontraditional ending. The film's eventual boxoffice success does not take away from its origins as a $1.35 million production. If the movie had earned only $5 million at the box office, it could still be considered commercial compared to its budget level.

In comparison, *The Blair Witch Project*, which earned $300 million worldwide and whose business plan (yes, they had one) called for raising $350,000, was always considered a commercial project. Audiences evidently liked it a lot; other filmmakers were more critical. But the filmmakers made the film they intended to make and were successful in their effort. Not only were they innovative in the filmmaking but also in their use of the Internet.

Defining "independent film" depends on the speaker's agenda. Filmmakers often want to ascribe exclusionary creative definitions to the term. When you go into the market to raise money from private investors (both domestic and foreign), it doesn't matter if your film is a mini-budget or a $75 million blockbuster. You are still finding your own financing. Sometimes filmmakers on panels declare that someone else's film is not independent by being "a genre" or "in a specific genre" (i.e., horror, comedy, family) used to drive me crazy. In the end, esoteric discussions don't really matter. We all have our own agendas. If you want to find financing for your film, however, I suggest embracing the broader definition of the term.

There are plenty of successful filmmakers who manage to find their own financing to do things their way—John Sayles, the Coen brothers, Jim Jarmusch, and Henry Jaglom, to name a few. They make films on whatever subjects please them. Their films may have a limited distribution, but the directors (who often are also the writers) have their own financing. They keep their budgets at levels comparable to the likely boxoffice receipts.

John Sayles has had many critical successes, such as *Return of the Secaucus Seven, Brother from Another Planet, Lone Star*, and *Sunshine State*. These films were financed by Sayles' own investors. The first big commercial hit was 1996's *Lone Star*. Similarly, the Coen brothers' independently made *Fargo* was their first major boxoffice winner, despite earlier critical successes such as *Raising Arizona*.

It seems to be a simple concept. If you produce a gizmo designed to lose money, you go out of business. Why would it be any different with a film? Many films lose money (ask the studios), but most filmmakers intend to have some success. Film investors have a right to expect to earn back their money, at least. Unfortunately, many auteur filmmakers find creativity and attracting an audience mutually exclusive. If you suffer from this malady, try to reeducate yourself. Even relatives have their limits. You are using other people's money. Be respectful of them.

Just as with feature films, investors often expect nonfiction films, such as documentaries and concert films, to make a profit. Sometimes it happens. These films have gained a strong presence at the theatrical box office in recent years. The success of *Roger and Me* in 1989 began the reemergence of the nonfiction film as a credible theatrical release. After a few successful films in the intervening years, 1994's *Hoop Dreams* attracted a lot of attention by reaching U.S. boxoffice receipts of $7.8 million with a budget of $800,000. The same year *Crumb* reached a total of $3 million on a budget of $300,000. In 1997, *When We Were Kings*, a documentary on the Muhammad Ali–George Foreman fight in Zaire 23 years ago, won an Academy Award. *Buena Vista Social Club*, made for $1.5 million and grossing $6.9 million, was nominated for the Oscar for Best Documentary. Michael Moore's 2002 *Bowling for Columbine* raised the bar for documentaries by winning the Oscar for Best Feature Documentary and the Special 55th Anniversary Award at Cannes. To-date the film has earned $31 million worldwide.

People Get the Money

A frequent question asked of me by students and clients is, "How much money have your business plans raised?" My answer is, "None. People raise money. Business plans are only a tool." Three of the best business plans I ever wrote are filed in drawers; they haven't raised any money. In addition, although you may have the most well-written and presented business plan ever done, to raise the money you have to (1) be ready to go ahead with the business, (2) understand the premise, and (3) be professional.

To be ready to get your project off the ground, you have to be focused on your goal. If you are arguing with your partners, are not ready to make decisions, or are unwilling to look for money, the quality of your business plan is immaterial. From the biggest consulting firms down to the smallest ones, there are plans stored on shelves gathering dust, because the client company was not ready to be serious about taking on partners or making changes. Business plans do not find money by themselves.

Once you track down your prey and deliver this terrific plan, you have to explain what it is all about—how it represents you. A plan is only a guideline with strategies and forecasts. You have to demonstrate to others that you can carry out the steps described within. Unless you understand every step of the plan—rather than just handing over a document written by someone else—you will not be able to do this.

Finally, are you adept at handling business in a professional and impressive manner? When all is said and done, the company is only a reflection of your demeanor and presentation. After all the numbers have been added up, investors are still betting on people. If they are unsure or wary about you, no checks will be written.

All consultants have clients that they would like to keep hidden. Sometimes it would be ideal if the entrepreneur and the investor never met. Some clients like to argue with investors and generally have a take-it-or-leave-it attitude. I once had a client who actually said to an investor, "I'm doing you a favor by giving you this opportunity. Take it or leave it." The investor left it.

Can Anybody Do This?

Developing a business plan involves the proverbial "10 percent inspiration and 90 percent perspiration." Anybody can do it.

Unfortunately, I have found that most people lose interest when faced with the amount of research and work that is required. If you want to make your own films, however, this is part of the price of admission.

To find financing for your films, you do not have to be part of the business world; you do not have to be an M.B.A. or an accounting genius. The business plan bridges the gap between right-brain creative thinking and left-brain math stuff. All it requires is the desire and a passion for the product. Being in control of your own destiny is a powerful enough motivation.

Hollywood Is Only an Attitude

This book does not restrict the term *filmmaker* to those toiling in the hills of Hollywood. Movie-making is a nationwide and worldwide event. The person in Cincinnati with a camcorder who aspires to make a documentary or a feature film is as much a filmmaker as his or her counterpart in Los Angeles. John Sayles lives and works in New Jersey. Watch the film festival rosters and you will quickly see that there is more movie-making going on outside of Southern California than in it. Consider the following example.

My client Rick Pamplin, who owns The Pamplin Film Company, lived and worked in Hollywood for a number of years. Rick sold projects to both studios and independent production companies, taught screenwriting, and produced and directed an independent film. Despite writing a screenplay that was released through Universal Studios, he found that "to do his own thing," he literally had to leave Hollywood proper and move to Orlando, Florida. We worked together to put his goals and objectives into a financial package. Rick says:

> The success of my company is directly tied to three things: a specific, written business plan, honest and direct communication with our investors, and our ability to make good-looking product on a small budget. When I began the company, I was a produced screenwriter and novice producer. Virtually no one would give me money, so I went to family, friends, and anyone who would listen. I raised small amounts of money, worked for low wages, and created commercial projects that would recoup easily. The first project—Michael Winslow Live—has run in multiple cycles on the Starz! and Black Starz! returning significant profit to its investors. The Pamplin Film Company has raised money for seven projects and is in preproduction on three features.

The moral of this story is that "Hollywood" is not a specific place. Living outside the environs of Los Angeles and New York is no longer a hindrance to success in this business. You need not be in those cities to meet the important players in the film industry. You might find them at a film festival or a film market, or simply at the other end of the phone.

No one has to travel anywhere these days. When fiberoptic technology arrived on the scene in the mid-1990s, its greater carrying capacity over coaxial cable made changes in how filmmakers worked. Fiberoptic allows a producer to be in one location and the background scenes, the actors, or both to be in other locations. In addition, the advent of digital technology allows people to be inserted into films at the touch of a button by the editor. This worries actors, who understandably prize control of their images. On the other hand, it improves on many old "blue screen" techniques for inserting the dinosaur to whom the actor appears to be speaking.

An Entrepreneur Is an Entrepreneur Is ...

For most entrepreneurs, the idea of boiling down a vision into a neatly contained business proposal is as foreign as the notion of taking a job. Nevertheless, the recipe for success in today's competitive business environment demands that we become managers as well as artists. The most common blunder that entrepreneurs make is to assume that a business plan is a creative piece of fiction you use to trick a bank officer into giving you money. Even worse is the assumption that creating a business plan is an interesting hobby for someone who has nothing else to do. The biggest mistake made by independent filmmakers is to see themselves not as business people but as artistes—creatures whose contact with the murky world of business is tangential to their filmmaking and unimportant. Nothing could be further from the truth.

When a person has an original idea and develops it into a product, an entrepreneur is born—a person who has personal drive, creates an intimate vision, and is willing to take risks. Entrepreneurs want to make the decisions and be in charge of the show; they want to do what they want to do when they want to do it! I have never met an entrepreneur who was not convinced that he was right, who did not believe that the world couldn't live without her film, and who did not want to control his own destiny. Independent filmmakers are the best kinds of entrepreneurs, because they want to push the edge of the envelope and seek new horizons. They are the major risk-takers.

Film investors are the biggest risk-takers of all, however. They bet their dollars on an idea and help it become a reality—a contribution not to be taken lightly. Too often filmmakers believe that investors should donate their money and then quietly go away. Of course, this attitude is not unique to filmmakers. Most entrepreneurs feel that their ideas have more value than the capital needed to make them a reality. Think again, or you won't see any cash.

WHY BOTHER WITH A BUSINESS PLAN?

The business plan is the entrepreneur's single most valuable document and her best safeguard for success. The majority of businesses that fail usually have paid little attention to proper planning. In Jake Eberts' book, *My Indecision Is Final: The Rise and Fall of Goldcrest Films,* he mentions several times that the company, which he founded, had no business plan. Although their first film, *Chariots of Fire,* won the Academy Award for Best Picture, the company (different from the one in operation today) did not succeed in the long run. Would Goldcrest have fared differently had there been a business plan? No one can say for sure, but it is obvious in reading Eberts' book that a group of very talented people got together with different professional and personal agendas. They also had very different business styles.

A business plan is a must for a new company (or an expanding one). It gives you the opportunity to develop a clear picture of the growth and bottom-line prospects for your film company. It enables you to make more effective decisions, and it helps everyone follow the leader. When you have a path laid out, you have guideposts to follow that will show you where you are vis-á-vis your goals. The secondary purpose of the business plan is to show the investor that you know what you are doing.

The ideal length and depth of a business plan varies from business to business. This is true if you are building a shoe factory or making *Nightmare on Elm Street 26*. You have something to accomplish and a specific path you must travel to accomplish it. The steps that you take along that path are defined in your plan.

Before beginning any business, you want to know the nature of your goals and objectives, the desired size of the company, the products and/or services it will sell, its customers and market niche, the amount of revenue likely to flow, and its sources. Whether you hope to start a full-fledged production company or just make one film, you have to identify who you are, where you are going, and how you are going to get there.

When you think of business plans, your first thought may be how to impress the investor. Before you worry about the bank or the distribution company or the wealthy investor, however, you have to make a personal business plan. For all of those people—and for yourself—you have to come up with an agreeable course of action, and you have to stick to it. This book will help you do that.

Do You Really Need a Business Plan?

Be honest with yourself. What is it that you really want to do? A full business plan is necessary for raising money for one film or a new company—not just to show potential investors what a "can't-miss" investment it is, but also to put on paper for yourself the direction of your work. It means being more than just a producer or director: it means planning ahead for three to five years for a company that will make a succession of films; it means optioning or writing enough properties to make the company valid; it means having around you a talented team to which you will delegate responsibility. Most of all, it means accepting responsibility for everything that goes on in the company, from the logo to the bank account.

Is This Book for Someone Making Only One Film?

In a word, "Yes." After three editions, people still call or e-mail and ask me that question. Any movie proposal—whether for a single film or a company—that seeks to raise money from private investors needs a business plan. If you are doing a single film, the outline is exactly the same, except you have fewer numbers to project and there is no separate overhead. The results of one film will take you out three years, from the beginning of development to 80 percent of your revenues being returned. It is essential to remember that before going into business, you must find out for yourself if business is your thing. One film is a business, and the producer (or executive producer) is the manager. You have the same responsibility to investors as if you were making four or five films. Going through this book will help you determine if a business is what you really want.

The Facts and Nothing But...

The structure for a business plan is standard, but the contents are not boilerplate. Each film company or project has its own unique qualities. All plans must be substantive, promotional, and succinct, with a length generally between 20 and 50 pages—that is, comprehensive but not too long. The most important aspect of business plans is that they contain enough information in a readable format that they excite, or at least impress, potential investors. Most of all, the plan should represent you and your ideas. Copying someone else's plan is like copying someone's test paper in school. You may give the right answers to the wrong questions.

A few years ago, a friend of mine wrote a business plan that was very professional and cleverly laid out. He found that he had to keep it under lock and key because other producers kept making copies of it. What they failed to recognize was the specialized nature of his company. It was structured to fund development money, not produce films. The payback to the investors is quite different with development money. The "borrowers" of the product were so enamored of the text and graphics that they were blind to the obvious: The business plan promoted a type of company that they did not plan to run. How they ever managed to explain the relatively low return to investors we will never know.

ABOUT THIS BOOK

Whether you use this book as a step-by-step guide for writing a plan or as a test of your own ability to be in business, it will help you meld creative thought with business fundamentals. It has been written in language that is accessible to those who are not skillful with business jargon. Understanding business is not that hard. Whether you want to take the time to learn about business, or even want to be bothered with the noncreative aspects of filmmaking, is another question. You will have to answer that for yourself.

What if, after reading this book, you decide you would be better off selling your script to a studio or directing for one? Have you wasted your money? No. You will have saved money by reading this book first. It is better to find out now, rather than several months or thousands of dollars down the road, that the business life is not for you.

Business Plan Outline

This book is best described as a movie within a movie. To find financing for your projects, you will have to describe how your company will function. Accordingly, this book describes the system of marketing and financing individual films within the greater framework of the film company.

The book is arranged so that the numbered chapters follow the steps of the business plan. They appear in the order that the sections of your plan should follow:

1. Executive Summary
2. The Company
3. The Films/Products
4. The Industry
5. The Markets and Marketing
6. Distribution
7. Financing
8. The Financial Plan

Finally, a sample business plan for a fictional company appears in Chapter 10. Note that the subheadings in these chapters do not have to appear in the business plan. This outline has been the stuff of business plans from time immemorial. No matter how independent you are, when writing your business plan, do not fool with tradition. You should make it as easy as you can for potential investors to read your plan. They are used to seeing the information in a certain way, so humor them. It is in your best interest not to be an auteur with your business plan.

As you devise your plan section by section, you will find yourself being repetitious; likewise, you will find the chapters of this book somewhat repetitious. Think of the plan as a series of building blocks. Starting with the second section, you will describe the members of your company and explain what you are all about. Next, you will talk about your products in exhaustive detail. Then, to set the background, you will describe the industry as a whole. Once you have set the milieu within which you function, you will show the market potential of your products. In the section on distribution, you will explain the methods and potential of issuing your products in the different markets. Finally, you will explain the financial methods and how the company is going to make money.

To put it another way, in the first few sections, you will explain *what* the company is; the rest of the plan will consist of all the *hows*. I skipped over the executive summary. As that is covered in the next chapter, I will not spoil the surprise. Suffice it to say that the first section of the plan is exactly what it says it is—a summary of everything else in the plan.

Goals of This Book

My goal in writing this book is to give you, the independent filmmaker, an introduction to the world of business and to provide a format to help you present yourself and your projects in the best possible light. There are many filmmakers with projects who are struggling to obtain equity (partnership) dollars. Being able to see your project from the investor's viewpoint and being able to present it to the financial community in a recognizable form will give you an useful edge on the competition.

Throughout the book, I emphasize that this is your plan. People want to know who *you* are and what you will do. Dreams are good; the nature of an entrepreneur is to be a dreamer. Your plan will bring the dream and the reality together.

SOMETHING NEW

This book contains a CD with additional information. Don't go to it until you have gone through the book. One of the many things that I have always wanted to do is explain the art of forecasting. Since the sample business plan is for a multiple film company, the exercises on the CD take one of the films from that company and explain how I arrived at the forecast and cash flow. Other information included are sample synopses of well-known films, sample distribution contracts, a list of sources for data information and film festivals that meet the Academy of Motion Picture Arts and Sciences eligibility rules for short films.

DISCLAIMER

To make the book clearer, many examples of business plans are presented. In some cases, I have quoted from existing business plans and indicate as much. In most cases, though, I have invented names of people, movies, and companies as a literary device. Given the number of production companies and movies that appear and disappear every day, I may accidentally have selected a name you use or propose to use. Such an occurrence is purely coincidental. Certain factual items in the text may be out of date by the time you read this book. What is important for you, however, is not the specifics, but the methodology.

Executive Summary

1

"Begin at the beginning," the King said, gravely, "and go till you come to the end; then stop."

LEWIS CARROLL
Alice's Adventures in Wonderland

READ THIS CHAPTER LAST!

This admonition is like saying, "Don't open this package until Christmas!" You are, right this minute, ignoring me and reading this chapter anyway. Fine, but when it comes to writing your business plan, write the Executive Summary last. Typically, investors will read The Executive Summary first; nevertheless, it is the section you want to write last. It is the hook that pulls readers into your net, and it must represent your future plans precisely.

The Executive Summary is the place where you tell readers what you're about to tell them. Am I confusing you? Remember that old advice about writing term papers: "Tell them what you're going to tell them; tell them; tell them what you told them?" You do the same thing with the Executive Summary. It is a condensed version of the rest of your proposal. This is not a term paper; this is your life.

The beginning of your work is the section about your film (or films if you are starting a multifilm company). You give a brief overview of the people, the products, and your goals. In the rest of the sections—Films, Industry, Markets, Distribution, and Finance—you give them more detail about how the company is going to function. The last section you write is the Executive

Summary, which is just that: a summary. It presents a review of the plan for the reader.

Why Write the Summary Last?

Developing a business plan is a process of discovery. Until you actually put your business plan together, you cannot be sure what it will contain. As you will see in reading the rest of this book, much research, thought, and skill goes into a proposal of this type. The total plan is the result of everything you learn from the process, and the Executive Summary is the culmination of that full effort.

The Executive Summary is written last for the same reason that you do a full budget before you do the top pages. You may have a problem with this comparison if you do the top pages of the budget first or if you do only the top pages. At best, filling in numbers on the top pages is a "guesstimate." Only when you actually work out the real 20 to 30 pages of the budget, based on the script breakdown, do you know the real costs.

Perhaps your guesstimate will end up being right on the mark. I don't think anyone has worked out the precise odds on that happening, but you might be more likely to win a lottery. A more probable scenario is that you will have backed yourself into a corner with original numbers that are too low. The real budget will turn out to be greater than your estimate by $500,000, $800,000, or even more. When that happens, your potential investors will be extremely unimpressed. If you are not sure how their money will be spent, ought they to trust you with it?

A business plan is the same situation magnified a thousand times. All the reasons outlined in the Introduction for writing a business plan come into play. You may be setting parameters for yourself that are unrealistic and that lock you into a plan you cannot carry out. In putting together the proposal, your investigation of the market may cause you to fine-tune your direction. Learning more about distribution—and we all can—may invite a reworking of your film's release strategies.

Even if you were inventing a fictional company, as I did in Chapter 10, the Executive Summary must be written last. I did not know what I was going to say in the summary until the rest of the plan was written. Although I invented the company and the statistics for the sake of an example, my industry, market (except for the cats), distribution, and finance sections are all real. I did not know which facts about all those elements would apply to my particular situation. Likewise, until I worked out the numbers and cash flows, I could not summarize the need for cash. The most difficult task for many entrepreneurs is resisting the impulse to write five quick pages and run it up the flagpole to see if anyone salutes. A business plan is not a script, and you cannot get away with handing in only a treatment. You must have your business plan well thought out, and you must present a complete package. Think of this as a rule. Other things are suggestions that you would be wise to follow, but this is definitely a rule. Go through the process first. By the time you have carefully crafted this document and gone through all the steps outlined in the book, you will be able to proceed with as few hitches as possible.

This decision has to be a cautious one, not a haphazard one. You want to be sure that this proposal makes business sense; you want to be able to meet any goals or verify any facts that you set forth. Passion does count. The film business is too hard and it takes too long to tackle projects if you do not have the passion for filmmaking. However, business facts are the glue that holds everything together in a tidy package.

Investors are the second reason that you write the Executive Summary only after you have carefully devised your business plan. Before you approach any money source, you want to be sure that your project is reasonable and rational. Potential investors did not accumulate their money by chance, and they are not likely to give you money on impulse. If you appear rash and impulsive, your 15 minutes of fame will run out before you know it. Treat them as intelligent people, even if you are approaching the stock broker's favorite group—widows and orphans. They'll have a business advisor who will read the proposal.

Once in a while, there is that exception to the rule. Someone will ask to see just the Executive Summary. However, five will get you ten that the next communication says, "Let me see the rest of the plan." That person means today—now. He or she assumes that there is a body of work supporting your summary; therefore, the summary and the complete proposal have to match. You do not want to have to tell potential investors that you will have the complete plan in a month. You will lose their trust. The same is true if you need to put together a business plan for a single film—and it does happen. Certain investors or equity groups will ask for a business plan. Have all the market explanations, facts, and figures at hand and in order.

STYLE OF THE EXECUTIVE SUMMARY

The image experts say that you have 30 seconds to make an impression, whether it is at a job interview, in a negotiation, or at your local party place on a Friday night. Your business plan has a similar amount of time. First impressions count; they will make the reader either want to read further or want to toss the proposal aside.

Cicero said that brevity is the charm of eloquence; this thought is good to keep in mind. In a few paragraphs, you must summarize the entire business plan to show the goals driving the business, the films, the essential market and distribution factors, and the major elements for the success of the business. Each of the chapters in the outline has its own summary. I know that it is hard to understand this repetition; students and clients ask about it all the time. That is why I keep coming back to it.

Earlier I said that the Executive Summary is the hook; you can also think of it as the bait that attracts the fish. You want the reader to be intrigued enough to read on. You need not try to rival John Grisham or Stephen King as a writer of thrillers or horror stories. You should not expect to keep readers on the edge of their seats.

Simply tell the salient points in the Executive Summary: less is more. If the Executive Summary of your plan is as long as this chapter, it is entirely too long. You can be long-winded later. All you want to do in this section is give your readers the facts with as little embellishment as possible. Remember that this is a business proposal, not a script.

LAYING OUT THE EXECUTIVE SUMMARY

Follow your outline when writing the Executive Summary. Give the basic information of each section with as little imagination as possible. Do not deviate from the path that you have already chosen. Anything you say here has to appear in more detail somewhere else in the proposal. Refer to the Executive Summary of the sample business plan (in Chapter 10) while reviewing how to lay out your own summary.

Overview

Typically, the first of the eight sections of the Executive Summary is called "Overview." However, you can call it "Strategic Overview of the Company" if you prefer. This section is the introduction to your business plan. It describes the outstanding elements of your goals and plans. From this section in our sample, readers know that the fictional company Crazed Consultant Films, International is passionate about cats and is devoted to making films about them. They also know how many films are planned, at what budgets, and over what period of time.

The Management Team

Although part of the company section, a mention of your management team should be added to the Executive Summary to give investors an idea of your team's experience and expertise. If you happen to be starting a company with a well-known person or even lesser-known people; you will want to put those names up front on the first page. Be sure, however, not to name anyone who has not agreed to be part of the project.

The Film(s)

In this section, give readers only the most important information about your proposed films. The synopses of your stories come later. In the sample business plan, I have noted that the planned films are related to a series of cat books and have suggested the tone of the stories. Indicate any notable attachments: director, producer, actors but save the bios to follow your synopsis in the longer section. Same rule about people applies here. Do not mention anyone who has not seen your film and indicated in writing, at least by a "Letter of Intent," that they are interested.

The Industry

Before describing your specific segment of the marketplace, it is necessary to give an overview of the industry. Just a short paragraph to show the current shape and financial growth of the industry will do. Include such things are the U.S. box office, worldwide box office, total admissions, and size of the independent film market.

The Market

In this section, you should give readers a feel for the markets for your films and other products. I have made the market section of the sample plan a little longer than usual to explain the reasoning behind CCFI's plan. Because these films are a little unusual, I have spelled out their target markets. You may have more than one product. In that case, you should devote at least one paragraph to each one. Readers know that all the necessary details will come later.

Distribution

This part of the Executive Summary deserves some detail. Simply saying, "We will get distribution," is not enough. Don't laugh. I've seen this in plans.

If you have distribution attached, give names here. Don't be shy. However, do be circumspect, as with the body of the plan. Only mention real companies from whom you have received actual written commitments. Phrases such as "We have interest from many companies to distribute our films" are public relations jargon. If potential investors think that they will find such meaningless generalizations in the rest of the plan, they may not read on.

If you are planning to self-distribute your film, mention it here. Hiding that fact until readers have worked their way through 20 pages of the business plan will not help you at all. State your reasons and describe in a few sentences your knowledge in the area of distribution.

Investment Opportunity and Financial Highlights

This section summarizes all the financial information in your plan. The first item to include is that all-important fact that hundreds of people leave out of their plans—how much money you want. Do not keep it a secret. The whole point of handing this plan to potential investors is to relieve them of a little of the green stuff. They know that; they just want to know how much.

Follow the amount with a summary of the projected profit and loss over the next five years (if it is a multifilm plan) to give readers an idea of when they will get their investment back. Even though you are starting films over five years, the following years appear in your cash flow. You want to calculate all the returns so it doesn't look like your company is losing money over time.

Notice that I continually use the words *projection, forecast,* and *estimate* throughout the financial sections. Always qualify any expressions of future gain with one of these three words.

NEGOTIATION STANCES

The first strategy that I suggest in negotiating with an investor is to leave the negotiation deal points out of this document altogether. By doing so, you keep yourself open for the best deal. Notice that the financial examples in the sample plan do not show a breakdown for the split with investors. They simply show the pretax dollars available for sharing. How the interested parties decide on equitable shares will depend on the number of parties involved, the type of entities involved, and proposals not foreseen by this plan. Even if you have an LLC or limited partnership which specifies shares, you may find an investor who wants to put in all the money. In this case, he will probably want to negotiate one on one with you and your attorney. Several of my clients have had this happen.

I advise my clients to hold their cards close to the vest and to let the other person go first. Even though you have determined your needs and expectations in advance, a situation may arise that you had not anticipated. For example, one group that I worked with assumed in advance that they were looking for an investor in the company as a whole. I convinced them to forego detailing this investment share in the document. In the beginning, equity investors for the whole amount were hard to find, but the filmmakers knew several people who would invest in individual films. This option was better for them in the end. They kept control of the company, as there were no new partners, and they found the resources for financing features on an individual basis.

The Investor Wants How Much?

It is always perplexing for creative people who have put their hearts and souls into a project to give away 50 percent or more to an investor. A common complaint is, "I'm doing all the work. Why should he get 50 percent?" Your decision has to be based on whether the amount of investment money is worth giving the investor that large a share of the profits. I cannot solve this question for you. Your priorities and goals are part of this decision.

A standard business plan ploy that seldom gets funded is the 70/30 or 60/40 split in your favor. There may be someone out there willing to take it—never say never—but chances are that you will give your business plan to a variety of people, so reserve the bargaining for the individual. If potential investors seem unsophisticated, you can try it. If you are lucky, they will only laugh. If you are unlucky, they will laugh while leaving the room. At least the thought is not written in stone in your Executive Summary.

Specialized Financial Instruments

If your company is a limited partnership, private placement, or limited liability company, the amount of ownership is set ahead of time in the prospectus. Many entrepreneurs think that the business plan and the prospectus are one and the same. The prospectus includes a business plan, but also much more. It is a registration statement document that has been worked on carefully by an attorney (I hope). It includes securities that are to be sold, arrangements for selling, discounts and commissions to dealers, subscription agreements, how monies are to be distributed, and responsibilities and rights of company management and investors. An attorney must do the customary legal explanations. Otherwise, you run the risk of unintentionally opening yourself to accusations of fraud. Even if you plan to use one of these business structures, I would keep the business plan a freestanding document. The business plan is part of the total package. Even though you want to do one of these financial methods, being able to circulate the plan separately could come in handy. You never know what opportunities may come your way.

The Company

2

To open a business is easy; to keep it open is difficult.

CHINESE PROVERB

STARTING IS EASY

To start a business, all you have to do is choose a name and have a phone; ergo, you are in business. To be successful, though, a business involves much more. A company, according to the *American College Dictionary*, is "a number of people united for a joint action ... a band, party, or troop of people." The lone screenwriter is an island of self-absorption; the filmmaker is king—long live the king! When she becomes the producer or director, though, she is running a business.

Running a business embodies a totally different set of skills. It is a special kind of collaboration in which dictatorship does not work. For a business to run successfully, everyone must agree on its purpose, direction, and method of operation. This goal requires a lot of planning and communication.

For the first edition of this book, I recounted my first seminar in which I started the day with a discourse on "Common Blunders in Business Planning." At the break, my assistant overheard someone say, "What is all this esoteric nonsense? We came here to find out where the investors are." To make my meaning clear, I start each full day seminar by putting a list of companies on the board. I asked the seminar participants to tell me what these companies had in common. After attempts by several attendees, one observant person finally recognized that they all had declared Chapter 11 (bankruptcy with reorganization of the business), Chapter 7 (bankruptcy with liquidation of the business) or shut the doors in some other way. Here is a more recent list:

- The Shooting Gallery
- Propaganda Films
- Kushner-Locke
- Next Wave Films
- Helkon Media AG
- Kinowelt Medien (German)
- FilmFour Ltd.
- Signpost Films (United Kingdom)
- Granada film (United Kingdom)
- And those many Internet entertainment sites, some of which were Z.com, iBlast, Stan Lee Media, Digital Entertainment Network and Pop.com.

The first reaction from independent producers was that these companies were all big and that somehow their size contributed to their downfall. In reality, the reason companies—whether big or small—fail is the same in either case: lack of planning. Anyone can have bad luck. Part of planning, however, is looking at the future result of current decisions. In doing this, you can build in ways of dealing with bad luck and other problems. Granted, some crises are beyond your control. A bank failure or the bankruptcy of a distributor, for example, is such an outside event. But careful planning can help you anticipate even these external occurrences.

The business plan diagrams a path for you to follow. Along the way, there may be forks in the road and new paths to take; flexibility in adjusting to such changing conditions is the key. On the other hand, taking every highway and byway that you see might take you in circles. In that case, you will never get a project completed and in the theaters. A balance is needed, therefore, between flexibility and rigidity. Planning provides this balance.

KNOW YOURSELF FIRST

When asked what they want to do, many filmmakers (or entrepreneurs of any stripe) reply either "I want to make money" or "I want to make films." There is nothing intrinsically wrong with either answer, but there are more questions to be considered. For example, what is the nature of the films you will make? What are you willing to do for money? And, ultimately, who are you?

Before characterizing your company for yourself or anyone else, make sure that you really know yourself. For example, one filmmaker told me that she intended to live and work in Georgia; she would make her films there and seek all money there. For her, this goal was nonnegotiable. This position may seem rigid to some people, but you have to know the lines you are not willing to cross.

Goals 101

Having and keeping a clear vision is important; it is as easy or as hard as you want to make it. Ensuring that you understand what you are truly about is the first step. A full course in Goals 101 would be too long to include here, but let's have a quick review of the basic principles with a minimum of academic jargon.

Setting goals merely means clearly stating your main purpose. Objectives are often shorter-term accomplishments aimed at helping you meet your main goal. For example, writing this book was my ultimate goal; teaching university classes was a short-term objective to help me reach my goal. I felt that the best way to establish credibility for a book contract was by teaching at UCLA. From the beginning, I knew that the pay would be low compared to consulting and other work; however, over the short term, the book was more important. Teaching at UCLA, then, became a greater priority than making lots of money.

Both the business and personal aspects of your life may mesh quite well, but any conflicts need to be reconciled at the beginning. Otherwise, those conflicts may interfere with your success in one or both areas. Covert agendas are sometimes good to use with competitors, but fooling yourself is downright dangerous.

Formulating Your Goals

Formulating your goals may seem complicated, but it involves just two simple but essential steps:

1. Take a meeting with yourself at the start. (In Los Angeles and New York, everyone "does lunch.") Think about your

plans, look at them, dream about them; then set out to test them against reality.

2. Write your plans down. Entrepreneurs love to declare that they can keep everything in their heads and do not have to write anything down. Big mistake! If your ideas are so clear, it will take you only a few minutes to commit them to paper. Anything you cannot explain clearly and concisely to yourself will not be clear to someone else. Writing down your goals allows you to see the target you are trying to hit. Then you can establish intermediate objectives or a realistic plan to accomplish these goals.

A word about money is in order. John D. Rockefeller said, "Mere money-making was never my goal" other successful executives have made similar statements. Many talk shows have brought together groups of entrepreneurs to find out what motivates them. They almost always identify making the product, negotiating the deal, or some other activity as their main motivation; the money followed when they did the things they liked. Do something that you enjoy, that you are passionate about, and that you are good at; then the money, according to many popular books, will follow.

Whether or not you become rich, I cannot stress too often that filmmaking is not an easy business. Be sure that it is the filmmaking that draws you—not just the tinsel, glitter, and high revenue prospects.

Personal Goals versus Business Goals

Finding fulfillment is an elusive goal. To start, you must list and prioritize your goals. Unless you know where you are heading, you will be severely hampered in making decisions as you walk down your path. People have both business and personal goals, so it is crucial to look at both categories.

First, take a look at your personal goals to make sure that you do not inadvertently overlook something you want. Your personal goals are your private desires, your plans about your lifestyle, the dreams that will bring a feeling of satisfaction outside of work. Can you identify your personal goals? What is important to you? Is it family? Church? Riding horses in Montana? Consider the pursuits and activities that you find meaningful. Decide which are important enough to leave time for outside of pursuing your business.

If the idea of personal objectives still perplexes you, take some time to think about it. Being passionate about films is one thing; having nothing else in your life is something else. Once you can identify your personal goals, continue on.

List your personal goals on a piece of paper, not in your head; writing in the margins of this book is permitted. Describe as many or as few goals as you want, as long as you have at least one. Here are some examples to help you get started:

1. Improve my standard of living
2. Live in Albuquerque, New Mexico
3. Work out with a fitness trainer on a regular basis
4. Spend time with my family

Now identify your filmmaking (i.e., business) goals. Again, make a list using the following examples as a guide:

1. Make inspirational films
2. Make low-budget action/adventure films
3. Win an Academy Award
4. Create a distribution company in four years

On another piece of paper, list both the personal goals and the business goals side by side; then rank them in order, with "1" representing the most important to you. Only you can set these priorities; there is no right or wrong way to do it. Once you have made the two lists, compare them. What conflicts do you see? How can you reconcile them? Accomplish this task, and you will be ready to write the story of your business.

GETTING IT ALL TOGETHER

Putting together the story (or script) of your company is like making a pitch to a studio or writing a *TV Guide* logline, only longer. You want to convince an unknown someone of the following: (1) you know exactly what you are going to do; (2) you are creating a marketable product; and (3) you have the ability to carry it off. Essentially, you are presenting the basic "plot" of your company. The difference is that a script provides conflicts and resolutions as plot points. By going through the previous writing exercise, you should have resolved any conflicts. "Just the facts, ma'am," as Sergeant Joe Friday would say.

Remember what your teacher taught you in high school English: who, what, when, where, why, and how. These questions are your guidelines for formatting the Company section of your business plan. Before you go any farther, ponder these questions:

- Why are you making films?
- Who are you?
- What films or other projects will you make?
- When will you get this show on the road?
- Where are your markets?
- How are you going to accomplish everything?

Note that the standard order is changed a bit. The *why* needs to come at the beginning to set the scene for the rest of the story.

Why?—The Opening Pitch

Now that you have listed your personal and business goals, you can identify the underlying aim of your company, known in corporate circles as the "mission statement." This statement describes your company's reasons for existence to you, your partners and managers, your employees, and, most of all, your money sources. It allows those marching forward with you to know whether you are all marching to the same drummer.

A major reason for company failure is lack of agreement on where the company is headed. A company is always a group project; there is far too much to accomplish for one person to do everything. The important thing is to ensure that company personnel do not go off in three or four different directions. Many companies that fail do so from lack of focus; you do not have to be one of them.

Do you have a specific philosophy? What do you want to do? Make the greatest films ever made? Make children's films? Make educational videos? Clearly define your philosophy for yourself and others. As long as people can identify with where you are heading, they will not get lost along the way.

When your philosophy or major goal is on paper, stand aside and take an objective look. Does this sound doable to you? Would it sound reasonable if someone else presented it to you? Most of all, would you take money out of your own pocket for it?

By the way, in writing up this description, you are not required to incorporate all your goals for the world to see. Your personal goals are yours alone—unless they affect the company significantly. Suppose, for example, that you are active in animal rights organizations. For that reason, you are adamant that no animals ever appear in your films. Everyone has the right to know about this dictum. It may affect scripts that have even innocuous animal scenes. Investors need to know about any major restrictions on your projects.

I am often approached by producers who have strong feelings about the source of investment money (how it was earned), or about certain countries to which they refuse to distribute their films. These countries always end up being major markets, so this credo strongly affects the company's potential revenue. Distributors do not like to give up lucrative markets, and investors do not like to give up potential profits. You have a right to your principles; just let people know what they are.

This brings us to a brief discussion about honesty. What if you intend to make, say, environmental films but fear that you will lose potential investors by being explicit? Should you keep your true plans to yourself? Should you claim to be making some other type of film, such as action/adventure? This question has come up in seminars and classes repeatedly. In one class, the following conversation took place:

STUDENT: If I tell them that I'm going to make environmental
    films, they won't give me the money.
L.L.: What are you going to tell them?
STUDENT: I won't tell them what kind of films I plan to make.
L.L.: You have to tell them something. No one is going to buy
    a pig in a poke.
STUDENT: I'll tell them that I'm going to make action films.
    Those always sell well.
L.L.: Then you would be lying to your own investors.
STUDENT: So? The idea is to get the money, isn't it?
L.L.: If lying doesn't bother you, how about fraud? The best case
    is they will take their money back. At the very worst, you
    can be liable for criminal penalties.
STUDENT: So?

You may think that I invented this conversation to make a point. I wish that I had. Unfortunately, it is a true story. Is it surprising that, at the same time, the university offered an ethics course, and no one signed up for it? My job is not to lecture anyone, although it is tempting. Your moral values are your own. Suffice it to say that fraud is not a good offense to commit, and most investors do not respond well to it.

Who?

By this time, you ought to know who you are, both personally and professionally. Now you can use the mission statement to define your company. Start the Company section of your business plan with a short statement that introduces the company. Give its history, ownership structure, and details of origin. Include the following in the statement:

1. Type of company: public or privately held, sole proprietor, partnership (general or limited), corporation (type), state and city origin
2. Names of principals owners (silent and/or active partners), officers

A beginning statement might be something like this:

AAA Productions is a newly formed California corporation whose officers are ___ , ___ , and ___ . Our principal purpose is the development and production of Hispanic-themed films as well as the employment of Hispanic actors in primary roles. Over the next four years, the Company plans to produce three independently-financed feature films. During recent years, the movie market has become more open to stories about ethnic groups. Films with Hispanic themes have led the way and proved that there is a market. We feel that the time is right and that the window of opportunity is open for low- to medium-budgeted motion pictures.

Not only has the writer said what films the company intends to make, but he or she has also identified a specific goal that is both professional and personal. The company's "principal purpose" describes its mission statement. It is closely tied to the personal beliefs and desires of members of the company. To make it more complete, the writer might also define what size budget he or she considers to be "low" or "medium."

What?

Mysteries do not work, except in scripts. The readers of your business plan want a straightforward summary of your intentions. To say that you will make films or videos without a discussion of content is not enough. What type of projects do you plan to do? In the Company section of the business plan, include a short recap of the projects you have planned. You will explain the individual projects in more detail later in the Product section. You should summarize all the areas and industries that your plan covers, such as the following:

1. Films, videos, television movies of the week (MOWs), multimedia projects, industrials
2. Budgets of planned projects
3. Number of projects over a particular period of time
4. Type of functions (development, production, distribution) in which the company will be involved

Rationality must intercede here. What you want to do and what you are most likely to get done may be two different things. In the pile of business plans from outside sources at my office, for example, a group stated that it planned to make 10 to 12 feature films a year with average budgets between $8 and $15 million. This undertaking is laudable for a major studio, but it may be questionable for even a large independent production company because of the quantity of resources—both money and people—involved. For this brand-new company, it was a foolish goal. No one in the company had ever made a film before. Even if someone had, consider the effort. The films would require more than $100 million in production costs alone in the first year, not to say anything about finding the staff, cast, and crew to make them. Is this an investment that you would view as "reasonable" for your hard-earned money?

Of course, people beat the odds every day. If entrepreneurs believed in the word "impossible," there would be no progress in the world. Nevertheless, you should weigh the scope of your venture against the experience of the people involved in it. If no one in your company has ever made a film, the odds are against your getting money for high budgets and multiple films per year. Aiming to produce one low-budget film the first year makes those odds a little better.

Experience producing or directing television programs, commercials, documentaries, music videos, and industrials is better than no experience at all; however, feature films are different in terms of time and budget. Being circumspect about the size of the feature budget in relation to your experience will not only impress investors but will also keep you from overextending your abilities.

With a one-film plan, you need only look ahead for three years (one for production, two more for revenue return). If you are starting a multi-film company, however, you must consider what your company will be five years hence. Analyze everything you plan to be doing over that time. If you plan to go into book publishing in year four, that goal needs to be part of your plan. Even plans to sell the company in five years must be mentioned. All of this is part of your projected bottom line. Although you may not know all the specifics, the size, scope, and type of your planned projects need to be stated.

Even if your company has been in business for a long time or the principals have considerable experience, never assume that readers have an intimate knowledge of your business. If your genre is the Western, for example, you might write something like this:

> *We plan to produce Western films that are similar to* Dances With Wolves, *except that the budgets will be under $5 million and the Indians will always be the heroes. Since there has not been a successful low-budget Western for several years, we feel that the genre is due to make a comeback.*

Treating the Indians as the heroes that they often were will attract a rich aficionado of American history to fund the film. Put in a line or two about the current status of Westerns (e.g., *Lone Star* takes place in the West, but is it a Western?), and show that some financially unsuccessful films might have done better at lower budgets.

Do not go into exhaustive detail. You will do that later. Remember that it is important in this document to keep the malarkey factor to a minimum. That does not mean that you cannot put in a little public relations, but leave your press clippings for the Appendix.

When?

In describing your project or company, you may have already stated how and when you began functioning as a company. You may have a great deal more to say, however. The majority of companies run by independent filmmakers are start-ups. If your company has only just begun, there may be a limited amount of information to state. Be clear about the current situation, whatever it is. You may still be someone else's employee, for example.

But be sure that you really are in business or ready to launch. Go ahead and file forms that may be necessary for your type of company, print business cards, and have an address (even if it is your home or a post office box).

Starting Steps

You have already taken the first step of starting a business—translating the entrepreneur's vision into a concrete plan of action. Next comes the practical process of actually setting up shop. You must create all those minutiae that say to prospective investors, "These people are really a going concern." Note the following checklist:

- Define the job descriptions of management.
- Determine the location and cost of offices.
- Have your stationery and business cards printed.
- Set up phones and a fax machine for easy communication.
- Arrange for professional guidance from an attorney and an accountant.
- Introduce yourself to your banker and set up a checking account.

A more important step is choosing your legal form of business. There is no one form that is best for everyone. When making this decision, consult with your attorney or accountant. The most common forms of business are the following:

1. A partnership is a business with two or more co-owners. It can be established with a fictitious business name.
2. A *corporation* is a separate entity apart from its owners. To establish a corporation, you must file papers with the state and pay an incorporation fee. The business's assets and liabilities are separate from those of its owners. For this reason, many people keep copyrights under their

own names. Then, if the corporation goes kaput, you still own the films, the company name, whatever.

3. A *Subchapter S corporation* has a limited number of shareholders and certain tax benefits that differ from those for a general corporation.
4. A *sole proprietorship* is owned by one person. It is easy to initiate and faces little regulation. The individual owner has all the control but all the responsibility as well. It is the normal state of doing business for consultants and others who mostly work alone.

If the formation of your business is dependent on raising money, be clear about this. Just be sure that you will be in a position and willing to give full attention to the company on receipt of the money. It is critical to show some preparation (this business plan is an example) before seeking investors.

Suppose you own a company that has had problems in the past. Don't be coy. Obviously, you need other people's money for some reason. Most investors will insist on full disclosure. They need to know the depth of the problems to overcome. If you have leftover equity owners from a previous incarnation or have imprudently spent money on cars, confess now. In the business plan, the sin of omission is as serious as the sin of commission.

You may find yourself in another situation. What if the company was in some other line of business before you bought it? The name is established, but the business has not yet functioned as an entertainment entity. On the other hand, you may have bought an operating film company that has been unsuccessful. Both circumstances add assets and credibility to your company. However, do not attempt to give the impression that the company was anything other than it actually was, or that it has made more money than it actually has.

Do not be afraid to state the facts. If a company made garbage cans before you bought it, say so. Investors want to know what they are getting into. Besides, being candid has its own rewards. People with money tend to know other people with money. Even if one prospect is not interested, his friend may be. So do not be afraid to tell him something he may not like. Eventually, he will find out anyway. You will lose not only an investor, but also the chance for him to recommend you to someone else. It is a small world, and the investing community is even smaller. Once you start getting a negative rap, it spreads quickly.

Where?

Potential investors want to know where you are going to sell your products and services. Although "worldwide" is a good thought, you should be more specific. If you are making your first independent film, it is not likely to have a $25-million budget. (If it does, please reconsider; you are not Miramax yet.) Let investors know if you expect distribution to take one or more of the following forms:

- Theatrical
- Specialty houses
- Ethnic communities
- Foreign markets
- Cable
- DVD
- Direct-to-video

There are many options to choose from. Your choice may be complicated if you plan to produce more than one type of product and have different selling philosophies for each. Remember that this section is an introductory statement, not a thesis. A short summary, such as the following one, is all you need.

The company's objectives are to:

1. Develop scripts with outside writers
2. Produce theatrical films with budgets from $1 to $5 million
3. Produce educational films for the health-care market
4. Make at least one movie directly for a cable network over the period
5. Explore overseas co-production and co-financing potential for the company
6. Distribute films through independent distribution companies

How?

Up to this point, you have essentially outlined everything your company proposes to accomplish. In the rest of the plan, you will describe each step in detail. Chapter 3, "The Films/Products," is a continuation of the *what*. It is an in-depth study of each of your projects. Chapters 4 to 8 describe the *how*. This is the central plot of your business plan. How do you fit into the industry? How will you identify your place in the market? How do distribution and financing work, and how will you pursue each one?

MANAGEMENT AND ORGANIZATION

Conclude this section of your business plan with a brief description of the people involved in your company and the organization of the key team members. This means writing just a paragraph or two for each. Save the six- or seven-page résumés for the appendix. How much of the organization you describe depends on the strength of the management team.

Maybe you'll be lucky and have a well-known former studio executive as part of your company. Perhaps your executives have business expertise in some industry other than film. Film track records are important, but management experience in other industries also counts. If no one in your company has ever made a film, find someone who has and sign that person up. If you have no one currently, describe the job position and make the commitment to have it filled by the time your financing arrives.

Follow the example of a company with some entertainment experience:

> *The primary strength of any company is its management team.*
> *XXX's two principals have extensive business and entertainment industry experience. Ms. Simply Marvelous is XXX's president. Most recently, she has worked with MNY Co. in both acquisitions and production. Among the films that she was responsible for are* Cat Cries at Sunset, Phantom of La Loggia, *and* Dreaded Consultants IV. *Ms. Marvelous will have overall responsibility for the company's operations and will serve as executive producer on all films.*
> *Ms. Freda Financial, Vice President, brings to XXX varied business and entertainment experience, including five years' experience in motion picture finance with the Add 'Em Up accounting firm. Previously, Ms. Financial worked in corporate planning for the health-care industry.*

If you have a writer-director who has no feature film experience, you might write something like this:

> *Mr. Self Consumed will be writing and directing our first two films. Mr. Consumed has directed commercials for 15 years. In addition, he has*

done promotions for the Big Time cable system. Last year he directed the romantic comedy short film, Louise Loves. *It was well received at several film festivals and won the critics' award at the Mainline Film Festival. His fifth feature screenplay is in development at Crazed Consultant Films.*

Make these descriptions long enough to include the essential information, but the less important details should go elsewhere. For example, Mr. Consumed's commercials and the companies for whom he worked can be listed on a résumé in the appendix. For the sake of your reader's sanity, however, do not create a 10-page listing of all of a director's commercials, even in the appendix.

Catch-22 Experience

What do you do when no one in the company has any experience? Tread very carefully. My advice is to attach someone who does. Why would any investor believe that you can make a film with no previous experience and no help?

The amount of skill expected is related to the budget as well as the genre of the planned film. Suppose you have decided to make a $25-million film for your first venture. You have written a script and are partnered with people with no film experience. They have financial or retail backgrounds, but no direct knowledge of film. Would you take $25 million out of your own pocket for this?

In certain circumstances, you can use the ploy of discussing below-the-line attachments of merit. Some clients of mine, for example, happened to have an Academy Award-nominated and Emmy-winning cinematographer committed to their projects. It was to their benefit to include him in the organizational descriptions, as the partners' filmmaking backgrounds were not overpowering. The cinematographer can be of great benefit to the director, as all producers know.

Be careful how you do this, though. You want to avoid making the production of your films look like a committee effort. One wannabe producer came to me with a plan for a company, or at least a first movie, with himself as executive producer. He planned to start with a $20-million film and felt that running the computer system at a production company was appropriate film experience. His explanation read as follows:

Mr. So and So has 25 years' experience working with computer systems, 10 of them at X & X Production Company. Mr. So and So will be the executive producer on all films. He has an experienced crew ready to work with him. These technicians have a combined experience of 105 years in the film business. If Mr. So and So has any questions, they will be able to help him.

This is a dangerous trap. Expecting that your inexperience will be covered by the experienced people working in various crew positions may backfire. The old saying, "A camel is a horse designed by a committee," is applicable here. The producer is the manager of the business and must make the final decisions; therefore, the person in this position must have a foundation of knowledge on which to draw. Investors expect to see people in charge who have some vague idea of what they are doing. When describing their experience, some people elaborate on the truth to a fault. When applying for a job of any kind, it is frequently tempting to stretch your bio a bit, if not to make it up out of whole cloth. Think carefully before you do this. Filmmakers often put their most creative efforts into writing the management summaries.

Compare the following real biography to the "elaborated" version that follows:

Real biography

Leonard Levison has worked as an assistant to the associate producer on *The Bell Rings*. Before that, Mr. Levison was a production associate on four films at Gotham Studios. He began his film career as an assistant to the associate producer.

"Elaborated" Business plan version

Leonard Levison produced the film, *The Bell Rings*. Prior to this project, he was co-producer on four films at Gotham Studios. He began his film career as an associate producer on various films.

"Exaggeration," you say? "Harmless public relations puffery," you add? This action is similar to the inflated income some people put down on a home loan application. You might assume that this is just the way things are done, but this action can come back to haunt you. A Los Angeles entertainment attorney told me about a court case in which the fictional management biographies of the filmmakers were the investor's sole reason for suing. He said that he "bet on people" and only read the Management section of the plan.

Try to be objective about the company that you are creating. The likelihood that an investor will give money to totally inexperienced filmmakers is less than for a group with a track record. No situation, as I have said, is impossible. The safer you can make the downside (chance of losing money) for the investors, the likelier it is that they will write you a check. No matter how emotionally involved an individual investor might be in the project, there is usually an objective green-eyeshade type sitting nearby, trying to make your plan fit her idea of a "reasonable" investment.

A Word about Partnerships

In forming a company, you may want to take on one or more partners. The usual makeup is two or three people who co-own a company and work full-time in it. Each one is personally liable for the others. It is quite common for good friends to become partners. Because of the relationship involved, many people in this situation often do not take the same care in doing business with friends that they would take with total strangers. No matter what the affinity with one another, agreements between people must be made and contracts signed. How many dear friends have you had at one time or another to whom you no longer speak?

A good partnership requires the presence of two contradictory elements. First, you and your partners must be very much alike so that your goals and objectives mesh. On the other hand, you must be very unlike and complementary in terms of expertise. Often, one partner is more cautious, the other more adventurous. Whether to form a partnership can be a difficult decision. As in many other situations, the best step is to list on paper the advantages and disadvantages of partnership and see how it works out. The following are sample examples.

First, the advantages:

1. I will have a measure of safety because it takes two to make any decision.
2. I will avoid the unremitting and lonely responsibility of doing everything by myself.
3. I will have a highly motivated co-worker, because she has a profit share in the company.

4. I will have knowledge and experience available to me that is different from my own.
5. I will have someone to share crises with.

Here are some reasons not to enter into a partnership:

1. The monetary rewards of ownership will be diluted.
2. I will not have total control.
3. I will have to share recognition at the Academy Awards.
4. My partner's poor judgment could hurt me and the company.
5. I will run the risk of a terrible falling-out with my partner.

LESS IS MORE

The Company section of your business plan not only summarizes the essential facts about your company, but is also an introduction to the rest of the business plan as well. It should be short and to the point. Prospective investors want to know the basics, which will be described in exhaustive detail throughout the rest of your proposal. Readers of this book's first and second editions, many of whom were writers, often have said that the phrase "less is more" was important to them. The following chapters will build on the foundation established here.

3

The Films

Why should people go out and pay money to see bad films,
when they can stay at home and see bad television for free?

SAMUEL GOLDWYN

Quoted in *The Observer*

PROJECT SCOPE

Theatrical films are the backbone of most filmmakers' business plans. As the industry changes, however, the potential for artistic expression is growing far beyond the notion of a single theatrical. In recent years, many filmmakers have successfully specialized in documentaries, commercials, industrials, educationals, or infomercials, as well as cable, video, and DVD productions.

Whatever the projects or products, all business ventures in which your company will participate over the next five years should be addressed in this section of the business plan. This chapter demonstrates how to describe your projects. It explains not only the amount of information that you need to include, but also what you should leave out. This part of the business plan gives you the opportunity to expound on all of the projects that your company will pursue.

How do you know what you will be doing five years from now? Undoubtedly, you know more about some planned projects than about others; some of you may not even have specific projects yet. For example, you may have a script to shoot next year, but may not have a clue about the script for a film planned four years down the road.

Nor can you know what delays may occur along the way. It is less important to be psychic than to be as accurate as possible in terms of intentions and timing. If circumstances alter the original plan, everyone involved will reevaluate it.

The Right to Know

As your partner, the investor has a right to know what activities are contemplated in order to make an informed decision. Several years ago, a young man came to me with a proposal to create a highly specialized series of films. He planned to sell them in a narrowly segmented market. The plan contained much discussion about the future success of his company, but the only description of the projects was the word "films." He cited an estimated population of millions that were going to see these unspecified films. Being the curious type, I asked him what kinds of films he planned to make. His answer was, "Good ones." I pressed on, trying to elicit more information. After all, he guaranteed that millions would clamor to see these films. He replied, "I'm not going to tell anybody anything. They might steal the idea. Besides, it's no one's business; all they need to know is that it's a good investment."

Don't laugh too loudly. This story is only one of many, and this young man's attitude is not unusual. "Films," as you may have realized by now, is not a sufficient description of your planned product. Putting yourself in the investor's shoes, how would this strike you? You would probably insist on knowing the content of these incredible films, who belonged to this guaranteed market, and how they were going to pay back your investment.

There are certainly a few real reasons that a filmmaker (or any other entrepreneur) might worry about revealing the details of a proposed project: (1) no identifiable plans exist; or (2) someone might steal the idea. Although theft of concept is not an unknown phenomenon, there is a difference between not telling the general public all about your plans and refusing to tell a potential money source. Prudent filmmakers refrain from describing script details in a loud voice at the local coffee shop or at a crowded party; they also resist the temptation to ask seven or eight friends to read their projects. However, the prudent do tell the right people enough information to prove the advisability of the investment.

Success in any business revolves around the product. In film, where all forward motion to the goal is content-driven, the story is crucial. To sell your projects, remember the refrain, "Story, story, story."

Hype has a place also, but it must take a back seat in the context of this plan. The trick is to do some jazzy selling around a solid idea. All the public relations in the world will not save a bad film.

From Chapter 2, "The Company," you know that the first goal for the business plan is to identify your future course of action. The second is to show investors how profitable your business will be. There is no way to forecast your success without specific ideas to evaluate. Does this mean that you must have all your scripts, directors, and stars in tow? Not necessarily, but you do need to have a framework. At the very least, for example, you want to know that you are going to produce X budgets and Y genres over a Z-year period. You must provide enough information to estimate revenues and give the investor a fighting chance to agree or disagree with your forecast.

The Facts and Nothing But

Think of this section of the business plan as a story you are telling, with factual material as the priority. Fantasies may play an important part in scriptwriting, but using wish lists in this document can present a problem. Confusing the issue by citing a cast that has never heard of the project or books you do not own may give investors the wrong idea. Whether you create a false impression by accident or on purpose, the result is the same. Investors negotiate contracts based on the information you provide. In the end, if all is not as you indicated, promises can be canceled and money withdrawn.

FILMS

When describing your film projects, the objective is to present a descriptive overview of all the critical particulars without going into excessive detail. You should disclose each project's assets (components that may add commercial value to the project) as well as any nonmonetary values that are important to the type of films you want to make.

Show and Tell

The trick is to tell enough to engage readers, but not so much that you risk losing them. As we go through the different elements, we'll attempt to draw a line between sufficient content and excessive wordiness. Readers who must wade through pages of information that is hard to follow will just go to sleep.

Writers of scripts, books, and other literary pieces have a tendency when writing nonfiction to create a stream of consciousness that is hard to follow. Fiction requires emotional and subjective content that will draw readers into the fictional world. Business writing—and nonfiction of any kind—requires simplicity and directness. Dr. Linda Seger, noted author of books on screenwriting, says:

> *Screenwriting is about being indirect; proposal writing is about being direct. While the object of good fiction writing is to be subtle, hide exposition, and present many ideas indirectly, good proposal writing insures that the audience is getting the information clearly and consciously.*

This is the reason why some genius invented the Appendix. In the business plan, it contains details that may be outside the simple and direct information formula. As you proceed through the following sections, you will get a clearer picture of what this means. There are no official rules as to how much information you ought to include. You can do anything you want, but bring your common sense into play, and always try to be alert to the reader's point of view.

Scripts

Disclose enough material about each script so that readers understand its value. A short synopsis is the usual format. In a paragraph or two, you can tell the essentials of the story and indicate the genre of the film.

A student once questioned whether or not to include the title of his script. He feared that someone would steal it because it was innovative and catchy. Whether or not to reveal the film's title must be your decision. More often, writers fear that someone will pirate their ideas rather than their titles.

The first step to take to protect yourself from possible theft of concept or story is to copyright your project. Most writers register their scripts with the Writers Guild of America. An even better procedure is to file for registration with the Library of Congress in Washington, D.C.

Once you have done this, you can prove that your story existed as of a particular date, and you can feel free to give it to others. Keep in mind that registration does not prevent theft; it just helps you prove ownership in the event of theft.

Unfortunately, you cannot copyright ideas themselves. Michael Donaldson, in his book *Clearance and Copyright*, says:

> *Copyright law only protects "expression of an idea that is fixed in a tangible form." This means that written words are protectable; the ideas behind them aren't. You can't copy something that is just an idea in the air.*

Keep your plot summary brief. The more complete plot treatment, which usually runs two to three typed pages, belongs in the Appendix. If included in the body of the business plan, it will break the flow of the story you are trying to tell by taking the reader too far afield. If readers need more than the plot synopsis you provide, they will ask you for the treatment or for the complete script. A reasonable plot summary might look like this:

Title: Boys Who Wreak Havoc

Four teenage boys decide to take over a small Wisconsin town. They kidnap the minister's daughter as a bargaining tool in their effort to make one of their members the mayor. Their attempt to control the population unites the townspeople, who, although previously selfish in their individual pursuits, come together to take back their town. The girl is saved without bloodshed, and peace reigns.

This paragraph tells enough about the story to give readers an idea of the type of film and the overall plot. It will be an action film (the title tells you that) with little violence ("without bloodshed"). Of course, the writer might have added a few more sentences to spell this out so that there would be no misunderstanding.

Include enough information to be sure that the reader does not misconstrue the type of film you plan to make. If the girl is raped or there is a nude scene, be sure to mention it. Failing to mention a scene that affects the nature of the film because you think potential investors might not like it is a sin of omission. If, for example, you have let your investor assume that you were making a PG-13-rated film and you know that it will be R-rated, your money source can object and sue for his or her money back.

What if you do not have specific scripts? State this up front. Even without scripts in hand, you can define your projects in terms of size and genres. You may be looking for development money to obtain scripts or to live on while you write them. Concentrate on what you know about your project. You must tell investors at least the size of the films that you plan to make. One way to describe this situation is as follows:

> *We are planning to make three films with family themes over the next five years, ranging in size from $1 million to $10 million. The initial $50,000 will allow the Company to develop scripts and to option stories from other writers. Production is expected to begin by the end of the first year after funding.*

This scenario is not as tempting to investors as the first one, but it is doable. For investors, providing money for development is always a greater risk than providing money for well-planned projects. The danger for the investor is that the producer may never find the right project and begin production. Or an agreement made with the source of production money may further dilute the initial investor's position. However, if you have some experience and a credible team, try for the development money.

What if you know neither the subject of your films nor the size of their budgets? In one plan, the company stated: "The producers plan to make low-budget features with the formula that has proved most profitable both in theatrical and video releases ... scripts in this area are plentiful." Seems a little vague, doesn't it? Aren't you curious to know what these proven formulas are?

Typically, the information in a proposal of this type is not enough. The right mix of ingredients is always a balancing act, but you probably would have to be a known filmmaker with an impressive track record to get away with this proposal. Even for an experienced moviemaker, this pitch would be hard to sell. Most people want to see specifics to which they can attach a value, either monetary or personal. Anyone with a modicum of business sense understands that handing out money to someone with no real plans except "to make a film" would appear to be foolish.

No doubt you can find an exception to this rule somewhere. Perhaps you've heard about an eager young filmmaker who, with his toothy smile and youthful enthusiasm, convinced a jaded deal-maker to hand over money. Nothing is impossible, but the odds are against this happening. This scenario sounds too much like a script and not enough like real life.

At this point, you may also want to address the question of the potential audience for your flick. It does not hurt to add a qualifying sentence to your plot synopsis—for example, "Films about Wisconsin, such as *Walter from Wisconsin* and *Cheeseheads Reign Supreme*, have been popular lately. We plan to capitalize on this phenomenon." On the other hand, you may be shooting the film in Wisconsin and raising your money there. In that case, add "Director Buffy Angel has close ties to the Milwaukee area, where the film will be shot." However, save the discussion of the distribution and financial ramifications of your films for later sections. If your readers follow custom, they will have read the Financial section before this one anyway. It is easiest for readers to follow your plan if you group all of the project descriptions together and do not digress to long discussions on other subjects.

ATTACHMENTS AND THEIR VALUE

In our balancing act, any person, place, or thing that adds value to the script is important. You want to give your project every chance to see the light of day, so recount any attachment with a perceptible value. Here are five examples of attachments: (1) option, (2) book, (3) star, (4) director, and (5) dollars. Keep in mind that your mother's opinion is not one of the choices.

Options

An option is a written agreement giving the producer exclusive rights to a project over some specific length of time. If the option is exclusive, it ensures that no one else can make the project while the producer holds the option. Obviously, if you are the writer, it is your project. However, if you are representing other writers' scripts as part of your package, you must declare the ownership status. Representing films as your own when they are not is clearly a no-no.

Not only the script itself, but also the subject may need an option. If you are dealing with true stories of living people (or deceased persons whose estates own the representation of their likeness and life), you may need to seek permission to do the story. Getting the option, or "rights," after the fact can be a costly process. You do not want to be in the position of having a deal on the table for a film and going back to obtain the rights to it. After the fact, the subject can and often will deny having given verbal permission. If you have not done your homework, it is the subject's right to stop the production, which sometimes leads to an expensive payoff or a court injunction.

Books

A published book adds value to a film in several ways. The sales history adds clout to your project, the specialized market it represents provides a ready-made audience, and the book usually furnishes additional ways to hype the film. Unless it is your book and copyright, the first step is—you guessed it—an option. The cost of the option depends, again, on the person you are dealing with and the relative fame of the book. It would be useless to even try to give you prices. As soon as the ink is dry in this book, the market will have changed. In truth, a book option, like a script option, can cost anywhere from nothing to millions of dollars.

An author (or the representatives of an estate) may have a subjective reason for you to make the book into a film and be very generous in making an agreement with you. On the other hand, if money up-front is the author's primary focus, he or she will drive as hard a bargain as possible. This area is one of the few in which your sparkling manner can have a concrete impact. On occasion deals have been done because the author liked the filmmaker and wanted to see the project get made. Passion for the project counts for a lot in negotiating with authors. One way to be sure that you cannot use the book, however, is to refrain from seeking the rights to it.

Options can be gotten at a reasonable price if the timing and people involved are right. Two producers bought the rights for a paperback mystery novel plus the author's next two books for a few thousand dollars. No one else had approached the author, and the books were not the type to make the best-seller lists. Nevertheless, the author had a large audience among mystery fans. With no competitive bidders, the producers were able to make a good deal.

Another producer optioned several books of women's stories. The books had a large following, but the subject was still "soft" at major studios. She couldn't get the deals that she wanted and the films deserved. Once *The Hours, Far From Heaven, My Big Fat Greek Wedding* and *All Women Have Curves* were released in the same year to critical acclaim and/or significant boxoffice results, however, studios and independent companies were falling all over themselves to make deals. It's all in the timing. A change in the attitude of the trendmakers (studio executives, agents, and critics) increased the value of the producer's optioned books immediately.

Being able to read manuscripts before they are published gives you an advantage over other filmmakers. Agents have access to unpublished manuscripts all the time. If you happen to know about a book that is about to be published by an unknown author and you can strike a deal prior to publication, it may work to your advantage financially.

Stars and Other Fantasy People

Attaching star actors, star directors, and famous producers is the fantasy of many independent filmmakers. Having Brad Pitt or Tom Hanks in your $500,000 film might be a recurrent dream of yours, but, unfortunately, their salaries have several more zeros. Nevertheless, you can have attachments that add value to your project, as long as they are real. No "wish" lists.

At this level, we are clearly not thinking of "bankable" stars (the actors whose names ensure a certain level of box office when the film opens), but you still can have a name that interests an investor. The value of the name is often in the eye of the beholder. Foreign buyers often put value on names that are only so-so on a U.S. movie marquee.

Directors who command high salaries will also be out of the reach of very low-budget filmmakers. Emphasize your director's previous experience, but do not fabricate it. With higher budgets (over $5 million), the inexperience of the director can become a hindrance and possibly dangerous. You want the director to be able to handle the film. In addition, experienced actors are often unwilling to work with an unseasoned director, and investors become more nervous about spending their money.

Because the producer has the major responsibility for keeping the budget on track, previous experience with feature films is important. In independent filmmaking, the producer is often the only connection between investors and their money. Once the cash has gone into the film's bank account, investors must depend on the producer to protect its use. Not only does the producer watch the money, but she has to have enough clout with the director to stop him from going over budget. Always keep in mind that this process is a balancing act of all the different elements.

Money

"Well," you say, "of course, money adds value." It seems redundant but really is not. Clearly, hard cash for development and production has a straightforward relationship to your project, but what about any partial funds attached to your project? For some reason, newer producers do not think to mention them as part of their product description, but they should. If any money at all is attached to your project, announce it here. You will discuss it at greater length in the Financing section. Remember that all attachments are part of the film's synopsis. You want to depict any ingredients of this mix that will positively influence someone to make your film. In addition to hard cash, you should mention any co-production agreements, below-the-line deals, negative pickups, or presales. But make sure you have your deals in writing before putting them in the business plan.

BUDGET—THE SHORT FORM

For prospective investors to evaluate your films completely, they need to know the size of the budget. Again, we have two types of films: those with complete scripts and those that are just a gleam in the producer's eye. When real scripts exist, real budgets should exist also.

To save money, many filmmakers pass a tuning fork over their script and say, "One million dollars." Do not just make up a figure. Anyone who contemplates financing your film will take this number seriously. So should you.

Many independent films have been delayed because the money ran out during either principal photography or post-production. The investors have said, "You told me $800,000, so that is all you are getting." Studios often have reserves for a certain amount of budget overruns; equity investors do not. This admonition also goes for digital filmmakers. Include enough money for transferring to 35 mm. (More about digital in Chapter 4, "The Industry".)

Some filmmakers develop only the two top sheets of the budget—this is just one step ahead of the tuning fork method—and figure out the complete cost later. Do it now to save explanations later. Estimating the cost of the general categories (cast, location, wardrobe, and so on) can be very dangerous, no matter how experienced you are. Break down the script (production managers, line producers are good at this job) and calculate the entire amount.

In describing your product, you should simply state the size of the budget along with its attachments. A paragraph or two on the entire project will be sufficient. Consider the following example:

> *This film has a $2-million budget, based on filming in Cincinnati. Susie Starstruck and Norman Goodlooking are set to star in the film. Ms. Starstruck has been featured in* The Gangbusters *and* Return of the Moths. *Mr. Good looking has appeared in several movies of the week. Herman Tyrant, the director, has made two low-budget films (*Be My Love *and* Girls Don't Sing*) and has previous experience in commercials. The film has partial financing of $100,000 from an equity investor, with all territories still free for distribution.*

In this paragraph, the writer has explained the essentials. From the preceding paragraph, we have learned the basic plot of the film. Here we learn the size of the budget, the location (much of the cost in this example is predicated on the film being shot in a right-to-work state), and the experience of the lead actors and director. One investor already has an equity position, but all the sales markets are available. Note that the writer has saved any discussion on the implications of adding another equity investor for the negotiation.

Do not worry about repetition; it is part of the building-block formula. You give an overview of the product. Then, in the Distribution and Financing sections, you go into greater detail about pertinent elements.

What if you do not have a full script or any actors and you have little or no experience? Do not lose heart. You can still explain what you are planning to do. Look at this example:

> *The ABC Company plans to make four films over the next five years. The first two films will be low-budget ($250,000 and $1 million, respectively)*

and will deal with coming-of-age themes. They are intended for distribution in specialty theaters. Both films are in the treatment stage, and the director, Fearless Author, will write the screenplays. Mr. Author wrote and directed four short films, two of which have won awards at film festivals. Mr. Experienced Producer, whose films include Growing Up? *and* Life Is a Flower, *has given us a letter of intent agreeing to serve as executive producer. The third and fourth films will be in the $3- to $5-million range. Mr. New Producer will produce these films after serving as co-producer on the first two. Neither treatments nor scripts exist for the third and fourth films. They will be in development during the first two years.*

Common sense will tell you that this package has less substance than the first one. It may be harder to find financing, but not impossible. If you find yourself in a similar situation, all you can do is try to create as many advantages for yourself as possible. The worst approach you can take is to say, "We are nobody with no plans. We plan to find no one experienced in anything, but we want your money anyway." It's true that no one is going to be this truthful, but on many proposals, it is not difficult to read these words between the lines. You have to learn to make realistic compromises to reach your goals. And above all, don't lie.

Too Much Can Be Harmful

One of the biggest nightmares that financial folks have is to receive a ten-pound business plan that includes every piece of paper in the producer's desk. Your goal is to have people read your proposal; therefore, you want to give them enough information without making the plan too heavy to lift. Suppose you have a complete budget for each of your projects. Do not put them anywhere in this business plan. An interested party will ask for them soon enough, and you can have the dubious thrill of explaining every last nickel. If you have a strong desire to show detail, you can put the top sheets of the budgets in your Appendix for perusal at the reader's convenience.

The same goes for the biographies of the stars, director, producer, and anyone else involved with your projects. A few paragraphs describing each principal's background is sufficient. The three-page bios do not need to be in the body of the plan. If you feel strongly that someone will have a burning need for this information, the Appendix is the place for it.

Don't make potential investors guess about the applicable credits by including newspaper reviews in your business plan.

Summarize the essentials. If you are bursting at the seams with your wonderful reviews, you know where they go—the Appendix. As far as I am concerned, photocopies of any kind should be forbidden by law to appear in business plans. When you are trying to separate investors from their money, a well-typed, neat page counts; it shows that you care enough to give them the very best.

One plan in my possession actually weighs in at two pounds. Thrown in with the appropriate and readable text are nine pages detailing every industrial and commercial film that the director made. Later sections include photocopies of numerous charts and articles from various publications. The investor is presumably supposed to wade through all this paper and reach a conclusion. Not wise. By filling your plan with extraneous paper, you might appear to be covering up an absence of fact, or you might give the impression that you do not understand the proposal yourself. Personal impressions are intangible, but they count. Always keep in mind that the human beings who read your treatise will have human failings. Once they are distracted or annoyed, their attention may be lost, and your package may be tossed in the "forget it" pile. Some rules are made to be broken, but the one about brevity and clarity is not.

NONTHEATRICAL FILMS

Markets exist for nontheatrical documentaries, direct-to-video, direct-to-DVD, direct-to-foreign, educationals, industrials, and other types of nontheatrical films. These categories are not as lucrative as theatrical film and its attendant ancillaries (video, cable, and foreign markets, for example), but it is possible to make a career from them. The educational film market has its own circuit. Distributors who specialize in this area often pay the filmmaker a percentage of the grosses, resulting in a small profit. A successful background in this format can help your cause. Several groups of neophyte feature producers have strategies to begin their independent feature film careers with educational films geared for the medical market. These can be made at a low cost ($5,000 and up), the subject is the star, and the production period is extremely short. No attachments are required, but if a famous doctor wants to appear at a reasonable price, do not turn her down. As with other products, anything that increases the sales value brings in more money.

The production of films intended to be direct-to-video or DVD, skipping theatrical release, closely resembles all the standards for quality of attachments for theatrical films. The potential for making money with these films is far different than for theatrical films. The lure of a breakout boxoffice success, such as *The Blair Witch Project* or *My Big Fat Greek Wedding*, does not exist, and there is no database to use for comparison. The ones that exist use theatrical releases. In addition, with the proliferation of products it is increasingly difficult to find space on retailer's shelves.

Many companies that used to specialize in this area have turned to features for U.S. theatrical distribution or gone out of business. Investors may not be as plentiful, but they are out there somewhere. The video market has weakened over time, but the DVD market is picking up. The dollars simply are shifting from one to the other. If you plan to start a company with only an ancillary market strategy, research and do the best job you can. Without a credible database, making a forecast is difficult. A case can be made to investors for the marginal profits.

Timing of These Products

Whether you are dealing with one product or several, being able to predict the sequence of events for production and sales has to be carefully charted over the next five years. Many companies are based on multiple products. Producers or their partners may come from other areas of the entertainment industry or from other businesses. It is not unusual for principals to use previously gained skills to start a company. In the case of multimedia, the producer may want to start with standard feature films and move into the new technology later on. Whether the chicken or the egg comes first depends on your objectives. Each product has its own purpose and its own natural place in the five-year time line. The sequence of events, however, should have some meaning rather than be haphazard. Often, filmmakers with backgrounds in documentaries, educational films, commercials, or industrials will start with those products to lay a financial groundwork for the company, then proceed to feature films two or three years down the road. The profits from these products can be used for part of the production cost of subsequent films, with the rest of the money being supplied from outside sources.

To launch any product takes thought and skill. If you can define the project, explain the market, and present logical financial information, you are on the right road. More often, producers with no experience in the nontheatrical field will add nontheatrical products to their business plan. For some reason, they assume that an inexpensive product resembling "real business" as compared to feature films is guaranteed to make money. They will explain this other endeavor with a simple statement, "This will bring a lot of money to the bottom line."

Any business that you enter into without enthusiasm or knowledge has built-in problems. Making a business successful is hard enough without the added burden of having no real interest in it. It requires extensive study to launch a product in any market. By the time you learn how a new business works, it may be too late for financial success. Rather than creating a miracle source of cash for films, you are likely to create huge debts. Worst of all, if you lose the initial funds, it may be difficult or impossible to raise more.

In combining different products along your five-year time line for the business plan, you want to keep in mind two questions:

1. How will these products work together?
2. What is the best use of the combined talents of the principals?

In one company that plans to begin with medical videos, one of the partners is a doctor. Her background as both a physician and a writer provides not only scripts for the videos but in-house quality control on accuracy. Presumably, she also knows the most efficient venues for distribution of the videos. This sounds good in concept. It is a smart move to go into a business in which you have previous work experience. However, the production of video differs from that of film in several important ways. It involves aspects of business not usually dealt with by producers, such as manufacturing, inventory control, warehousing, consumer advertising, and retail marketing and pricing.

Experienced business judgment helps. Running a commercial production company, for example, is different from being a producer or director at one. This type of company often has a chief executive and follows a typical bureaucratic structure with multiple vice-presidents, similar to the structure of the studios. Rather than being involved in the creative side of the business, these executives keep all the business balls in the air and the profit margins on track.

Whether a product begins the company, is sold concurrently with other products, or appears by itself at a later time depends entirely on the overall picture. The critical element for your business plan is showing that you know how all the pieces fit together. Each project essentially has its own mini-plan, with an analysis of the market, the industry, and finances. When you fit all the projects together, you have the plan for the whole company. At the end of the day, there has to be one bottom line for the whole package.

ASSESSING STRENGTHS AND WEAKNESSES

Casting an unbiased eye over your plans is always hard for entrepreneurs. A strong desire for everything to work often clouds your vision. Evaluating the strengths and weaknesses of your project(s) in the beginning, however, will save time, turmoil, and money later. You might be able to describe the strengths of your company as follows:

- Associates of the company possess unique skills or experience.
- The distinctive characteristics of our projects set them apart from our competitors' products.
- We have special relationships with distributors or other professionals or companies in related fields.
- Unique aspects of this business that will help us are …

Film production companies are often started with a combination of production and distribution personnel with varying levels of experience. Newer filmmakers team with experienced hands-on producers outside the company. Well-established companies often seek experienced personnel when going into new lines of endeavor. New Line Cinema, for example, grew into a major independent production and distribution company with low-budget, mass-market products, such as the *Nightmare on Elm Street* (1984) films and *Teenage Mutant Ninja Turtles*. Then they established Fine Line, a specialty division that made niche films. Skip into the next century, and the company was instrumental in that fantastic $300 million trilogy known as *Lord of the Rings*.

On the reverse side of the ledger are your company's weaknesses. Be honest with yourself when identifying your company's failings. This exercise saves many companies from later failure. By converting the strength statements to negative statements, you can spot problems. Write them down on a piece of paper to review:

- No one in this company possesses unique skills or experience.
- Our projects have no distinctive characteristics that set them apart from our competitors' products.
- We have no special relationships with distributors or other professionals in related fields.
- There are no other unique aspects of this business that will help us in any way.

Being good in one area of business does not guarantee success in another. For example, suppose an entrepreneur from one area of entertainment, such as commercials, decides to go into theatricals, an area in which he has no experience. Although he knows how to manage a profitable business, feature filmmaking has its own unique set of concerns. The business requires larger sums of money per project than do commercials and involves greater risks in terms of market. Commercials are done on order from a customer; feature films are made on speculation of finding a customer. In addition, designing a good commercial is not related to knowing what makes a good script. Successful executives often rush into new businesses without preparing properly. Used to calling all the shots, they may have trouble delegating authority or may hire lower-level development personnel rather than experienced producers in order to maintain control. The producer can counter these weaknesses by studying the new industry first and hiring seasoned film people.

Running through this exercise will help you in two ways. First, you will find out where the holes in the dike are so that you can plug them before any leaks occur. Second, you can use it to assess how much confidence you or anyone else can have in your organization. In addition, pointing out the obvious to readers never hurts. You should not make readers work to see the good points. As to weaknesses, most investors are sophisticated executives and will see the problems themselves. If you do not mention how you will overcome the obstacles your company faces, the investor may question your ability to understand them. Being frank may help your cause rather than hurt it.

START SMALL AND THINK BIG

Since the first edition of this book, Business Strategies has worked with filmmakers with all kinds of experience from none to thirty years. Trying to have a startup company with more than one product is difficult. Often clients want to do films, distribution, videogames, and music—all at the same time. My advice is to start small and expand as the company is successful. Make a few films first, then start your own distribution division or become a developer of videogames. For a new company, you need to have focus. An array of products stretches everyone's attention and energy.

The same advice goes to people who want to create a film company with 10 to 15 films in the first five years. A business plan is great; but, the word "plan" is operative here. The new owner doesn't know for sure how long it will take to be up and running. In addition, running a company as opposed to being a studio producer or an independent working on one film at a time requires different skills. New Line has been in business over twenty years. The Weinstein brothers (who many clients want to emulate) started Miramax as a small domestic distributor in the 1980s. Many successful years later the company became the 800-pound gorilla it is today. The point is that these companies started small and grew to multiple films per year and assorted ancillary divisions through making profits over time.

4

The Industry

The cinema is an invention without a future.

LOUIS LUMIERE

Moving images had existed before. Shadows created by holding various types of objects (puppets, hands, carved models) before a light were produced on screens all over the world. This type of entertainment, which most likely originated in Asia with puppets, was also popular in Europe and the United States. Then the Lumiere brothers created the cinematograph, an early form of moving camera, in Paris in the late 1800s. Little did they know.

Next came Thomas Alva Edison with his kinetograph, and shortly thereafter, the motion picture industry was born. Edison invented the first camera that would photograph moving images in the 1890s. Even Edison did not have a monopoly on moving pictures for long. Little theaters sprang up as soon as the technology appeared. In 1903, Edison exhibited the first narrative film, *The Great Train Robbery*. Seeing this film presumably inspired Carl Laemmle to open a nickelodeon, and thus the founder of Universal Studios became one of the first "independents" in the film business. Edison and the equipment manufacturers banded together to control the patents that existed for photographing, developing, and printing movies. Laemmle decided to ignore them and go into independent production. After several long trials, Laemmle won the first movie industry antitrust suit and formed Independent Moving Pictures Company of America. He was one of several trailblazers who formed start-up companies that would eventually become major studios. As is true in many industries, the radical upstarts who brought change eventually became the conservative guardians of the status quo.

61

Looking at history is essential for putting your own company in perspective. Each industry has its own periods of growth, stagnation, and change. As this cycling occurs, companies move in and out of the system. Not much has changed since the early 1900s. Major studios are still trying to call the shots for the film industry, and thousands of small producers and directors are constantly swimming against the tide.

IDENTIFYING YOUR INDUSTRY SEGMENT

Industry analysis is important for two reasons. First, it tests your knowledge of how the system functions and operates. Second, it reassures potential partners and associates that you understand the environment within which the company must function. As noted above, no company works in a vacuum. Each is part of a broader collection of companies, large and small, that make the same or similar products, or deliver the same or similar services. The independent filmmaker (you) and the multinational conglomerate (most studios) operate in the same general ballpark.

Film production is somewhat different when looked at from the varied viewpoints of craftspeople, accountants, and producers. All of these people are part of the film industry, but they represent different aspects of it. Likewise, the sales specifications and methods for companies such as Panavision, which makes cameras, and Kodak, which makes film stock, are different not only from each other, but also from the act of production. Clearly, you are not going to make a movie without cameras and film (or video), but these companies represent manufacturing concerns. Their business operations function in a dissimilar manner, therefore, from filmmaking itself.

When writing the Industry section of your business plan, narrow your discussion of motion pictures to the process of production and distribution of a film, and focus on the continuum from box office to the ancillary (secondary) markets. Within this framework, you must also differentiate among various types of movies. Making the $300 million 35 mm *Lord of the Rings* trilogy is not the same as producing the $150,000 digital movie *Tadpole*. A film (note that most people still refer to digital movies as "films") that requires extensive computer-generated special effects is different from one with a character-driven plot. Each has specific production, marketing, and distribution challenges, and they have to be handled in different ways. Once you characterize the industry as a whole, you should discuss the area that applies specifically to your product.

In your discussion of the motion picture industry, remember that nontheatrical distribution—that is, video, DVD, cable, pay-per-view, the Internet, and domestic and foreign television—are part of the secondary revenue system for films. Each one is an industry in itself. However, they affect your business plan in terms of their potential as a revenue source.

Suppose you plan to start a company that will supply films specifically for cable or the video/DVD market. Or you plan to mix these products with producing theatrical films. You will need to create separate industry descriptions for both types of films. Television has a different industry model from the video industry, which in turn differs from music. This book focuses on theatrically-distributed films, but the outline of the business plan is the same.

A LITTLE KNOWLEDGE CAN BE DANGEROUS

You can only guess what misinformation and false assumptions about the film industry the readers of your business plan will have. Just the words *film* and *marketing* create all sorts of images. Your prospective investors might be financial wizards who have made a ton of money in other businesses, but they will probably be uneducated in the finer workings of film production, distribution, and marketing. One of the biggest problems with new film investors, for example, is that they may expect you to have a contract signed by the star or the actual completion bond guarantee in hand before financing. They do not know that the money must at least be in an escrow account before either of these contracts is generated. Therefore, it is necessary to take investors by the hand and explain the film business to them.

You must always assume that the investors have no previous knowledge of this industry. Things are changing and moving all the time, so you must take the time to be sure that everyone involved has the same facts. It is essential that your narrative show how the industry as a whole works, where you fit into that picture, and how the segment of independent film operates. Even entrepreneurs with film backgrounds may need some help. People within the film business may know how one segment works, but not another. As noted in Chapter 3, "The Films/Products," it can be tricky moving from a studio or large production company to an independent or specialty house. The studio is a protected environment. The precise job of a studio producer is quite simple: make the film. Other specialists within the studio system concentrate on the marketing, distribution, and overall financial strategies. Therefore, a producer working with a studio movie does not necessarily have to be concerned with the business of the industry as a whole.

Likewise, foreign entertainment and movie executives may also be naive about the ins and outs of the American film industry. The history of Universal Studios proves that. In 1990, Japanese conglomerate Matsushita Electric Industrial Co. bought MCA Inc., the parent company of Universal Pictures. After five years of turmoil and disappointing results, they sold MCA/Universal to Canada's Seagram in 1994, which sold it to French communications/water company Vivendi in 2000. As we go to press, General Electric is negotiating to buy Universal from Vivendi. Some foreign companies have hired consultants to do in-depth analyses of certain U.S. films in order to understand what box office and distribution mean in this country. My experience has shown that foreign executives know how the industry works in their own countries, but are often confused about how it functions in the United States. As you go through this chapter, think about what your prospective investor wants to know. When you write your plan, answer the following questions:

- how does the film industry work?
- what is the future of the industry?
- what role will my company play in the industry?

The rest of this chapter compares studio and independent motion picture production. It also provides some general facts about production and exhibition.

MOTION PICTURE PRODUCTION AND THE STUDIOS

Originally, there were the "Big Six" studio dynasties: Warner Brothers (now part of AOL Time Warner), Twentieth Century Fox (now owned by Rupert Murdoch), Paramount (now owned by

Viacom), MCA/Universal (stay tuned), Metro-Goldwyn-Mayer (currently owned by Kirk Kerkorian and known as MGM/UA), and Columbia (now Sony Pictures Entertainment). After the Big Six came The Walt Disney Company. Together, these studios are referred to as "the Majors." Although the individual power of each has changed over the years (in recent years, MGM/UA has acquired more films than it has produced), these studios still set the standard for the larger films.

Until the introduction and development of television for mass consumption in the 1950s, these few studios were responsible for the largest segment of entertainment available to the public. The advent of another major medium changed the face of the industry and lessened the studios' grip on the entertainment market. At the same time, a series of Supreme Court decisions forced the studios to disengage from open ownership of movie theaters. The appearance of video in the 1970s changed the balance once again. Digitally recorded movies, which may be the next big paradigm shift, are discussed at the end of this chapter.

How It Works

Today's motion picture industry is a constantly changing and multifaceted business that consists of two principal activities: production and distribution. Production, described in this section, involves the developing, financing, and making of motion pictures. Any overview of this complex process necessarily involves simplification. The following is a brief explanation of how the industry works.

The classic "studio" picture was characterized as one costing more than $10 million. Now the threshold has moved, as foreign money has moved into bigger budgets. Most high-budget films need the backup a studio can give them. In addition, a studio is often in a better position to take a chance on a borderline film. It spreads its risk over 15 to 20 films. As long as a studio's failures occur with the lower-budget films and the successes are with the higher-budget films, the company is still in business.

The independent investor, on the other hand, has to sink or swim with just one film. It is certainly true that independently financed films made by experienced producers with budgets of more than $10 million are being bankrolled by production companies with consortiums of foreign investors, but for one entity to take that kind of risk on a single film is not the rule. Just to recoup the investment on even a $10 million film requires at least a $25-million box office. (Studios roughly estimate a breakeven boxoffice total by multiplying 2.5 times the production costs.)

At a studio, a film usually begins in one of two ways. The first method starts with a concept (story idea) from a studio executive, a known writer, or a producer who makes the well-known "30-second pitch." The concept goes into development, and the producers hire scriptwriters. Many executives prefer to work this way. In the second method, a script or book is presented to the studio by an agent or an attorney for the producer and put into development. The script is polished and the budget determined. The nature of the deal made depends, of course, on the attachments that came with the concept or script. Note that the inception of development does not guarantee production, because the studio may have many projects on the lot at one time. A project may be changed significantly or even canceled during development.

The next step in the process is preproduction. If talent was not obtained during development, commitments are sought during preproduction. The process is usually more intensive because the project has probably been "green-lighted" (more importantly, given funding to start production). The craftspeople (the "below-the-line" personnel) are hired and contracts are finalized and signed. Despite recent press reports to the contrary, producers do strive to have all their contracts in place before filming begins. The filming of a motion picture, called "principal photography," takes from 12 to 26 weeks, although major cast members may not be used for the entire period. Once a film has reached this stage, the studio is unlikely to shut down the production. Even if the picture goes over budget, the studio will usually find a way to complete it.

After principal photography, postproduction begins. This period used to require 6 to 9 months, but might be much shorter for some films today, thanks to recent technological developments.

Tracking the Studio Dollar

Revenues are derived from the exhibition of the film throughout the world in theaters and through various ancillary outlets. Studios have their own in-house marketing and distribution arms for the worldwide licensing of their products. Because all of the expenses of a film—development, preproduction, production, postproduction, and distribution—are controlled by one corporate body, the accounting is extremely complex.

Much has been written about the pros and cons of nurturing a film through the studio system. From the standpoint of a profit participant, studio accounting is often a curious process. One producer has likened the process of studio filmmaking to taking a cab to work, letting it go, and having it come back at night with the meter still running. On the other hand, the studios make a big investment. They provide the money to make the film, and they naturally seek to maximize their return.

If your film is marketed and distributed by a studio, how much of each ticket sale can you expect to receive? Table 4.1 provides a general overview of what happens when a finished film is sent to an exhibitor. The table traces the $10.00 that a viewer pays to see a film. On average, half of that money stays with the theater owner, and half is returned to the distribution arm of the studio. It is possible for studios to get a better deal, but a 50 percent share is most common. The split is based on boxoffice revenue only; the exhibitor keeps all the revenue from popcorn, candy, and soft drinks.

For all intents and purposes, the distribution division of a studio is treated like a separate company in terms of its handling of your film. You are charged a distribution fee, generally 30 to 40 percent, for the division's efforts in marketing the film. Because

TABLE 4.1
Tracking the studio dollar ($)

Your Boxoffice Dollar	$10.00
Exhibitor Share (50%)	$5.00
Studio Share (50%)	$5.00
Studio Share (50%—see above)	$5.00
minus distribution fee (50% of $5.00)	$2.50
	$2.50
minus overhead fee (12% of $5.00)	$0.60
Amount left to apply toward film negative (38% of $5.00)	$1.90
(does not include interest charges)	

Note: This example is based on average results. An individual film may differ in actual percentages.

the studio controls the project, it decides the amount of this fee. In Table 4.1, the distribution fee is 50 percent of the studio's share of the ticket sale, or $2.50.

Next comes the hardest number to estimate: the film's share of the studio's overhead. "Overhead" is all of the studio's fixed costs—that is, the money the studio spends that is not directly chargeable to a particular film. The salaries for management, secretaries, commissary employees, maintenance staff, accountants, and all other employees who service the entire company are included in overhead. A percentage system (usually based on revenues) is used to determine a particular film's share of overhead expenses.

It should be noted that the studios did not make up this system; it is standard business practice. At all companies, the non-revenue-producing departments are "costed" against the revenue-producing departments, determining the profit line of individual divisions. A department's revenue is taken as a percentage of the total company revenue. That percentage is used to determine how much of the total overhead cost the individual department needs to absorb.

In Table 4.1, a fixed percentage is used to determine the overhead fee. Note that it is a percentage of the total rentals that come back to the studio. Thus, the 12 percent fee is taken on the $5.00, rather than on the amount left after the distribution fee has been subtracted. In other words, when it is useful, the distribution division is a separate company to which you are paying money. Using that logic, you should be charged 12 percent of $2.50, but, alas, it doesn't work that way.

Now you are down to a return of $1.90, or 38 percent of the original $5.00, to help pay off the negative cost. During the production, the studio treats the money spent on the negative cost as a loan and charges you bank rates for the money (prime rate plus one to three percentage points). That interest is added to the negative cost of your film, creating an additional amount above your negative cost to be paid before a positive net profit is reached.

We have yet to touch on the idea of stars and directors receiving gross points, a percentage of the studio's gross dollar (e.g., the $5.00 studio share of the total boxoffice dollar in Table 4.1). Even if the points are paid on "first dollar," the reference is only to studio share. With several gross point participants, it is not unusual for a boxoffice hit to show a net loss for the bottom line.

Studio Pros and Cons

When deciding whether to be independent or to make a film within the studio system, the filmmaker has serious options to weigh. The studio provides an arena for healthy budgets and offers plenty of staff to use as a resource during the entire process, from development through postproduction. Unless an extreme budget overrun occurs, the producer and director do not have to worry about running out of funds. In addition, the amount of product being produced at the studio gives the executives tremendous clout with agents and stars. The studio has a mass distribution system that is capable of putting a film on more than 3,000 screens for the opening weekend if the budget and theme warrant it. *Harry Potter and the Chamber of Secrets*, for example, opened on 3,682 screens. Finally, the director of a studio film need not know anything about business beyond the budget of the film. All the other business activities are conducted by experienced personnel at the studio.

On the other hand, the studio has total control over the filmmaking process. Should studio executives choose to exercise this option, they can fire anyone and hire anyone they wish. Once the project enters the studio system, the original screenwriters may not even see their names listed under that category on the screen. The studio may hire additional writers. For example, the original co-writers of *The Last Action Hero* asked for an arbitration hearing with the Writers Guild because the studio did not give them screenwriting credit. The Writers Guild awarded them "story by" credit, but the screenwriting credit remained with the later writers. Generally, the studio gets final cut privileges as well.

No matter who you are or how you are attached to a project, once the film gets to the studio, you can be negotiated to a lower position or off the project altogether. The studio is the investor, and it calls the shots. If you are a new producer, the probability is high that studio executives will want their own producer on the project.

Those who want to understand more about the studio system should rent Christopher Guest's film *The Big Picture* or Robert Altman's *The Player* and read William Goldman's books *Adventures in the Screen Trade* and his year 2000 sequel *Which Lie Did I Tell?: More Adventures in the Screen Trade*. The studios are filled with major and minor executives in place between the corporate office and film production. There are executive vice-presidents, senior vice-presidents, and plain old vice-presidents. Your picture can be green-lighted by one executive, then go into turnaround with her replacement. Getting decisions made is a hazardous journey, and the cliché, "No one gets in trouble by saying no," proves to be true more often than not.

MOTION PICTURE PRODUCTION AND THE INDEPENDENTS

What do we actually mean by the term "independent"? Defining "independent film" depends on whether you want to include or exclude. Filmmakers often want to ascribe exclusionary creative definitions to the term. When you go into the market to raise money from investors (both domestic and foreign), however, being inclusive is much more useful. If you can tell potential investors that the North American box office for independent films in 2002 was $3.4 billion, they are more likely to want a piece of the action. The traditional definition is a film that finds its production financing outside of the studios and is free of studio creative control. The filmmaker obtains the negative cost from other sources. This is the definition of independent film used in this book, regardless of who the distributor is. Likewise, AFMA (formerly the American Film Marketing Association) defines an independent film as made or distributed by "those companies and individuals apart from the major studios that assume the majority of the financial risk for a production and control its exploitation in the majority of the world." In the end, esoteric discussions don't really matter. We all have our own agendas. If you want to find financing for your film, however, I suggest embracing the broadest definition of the term.

When four Best Picture Oscar nominations went to independent films in 1997, reporters suddenly decided that the distributor was the defining element. Not so. A realignment of companies that began in 1993 has caused the structure of the industry to change at a faster pace than before. And a surge in relatively "mega" profits from low-budget films (production costs under $10 million) has encouraged the establishment of "independent" divisions at the studios. By acquiring or creating these divisions, the studios handle more films made by producers using financing from other sources. Disney, for example, purchased Miramax Films, maintaining it as an autonomous division. New Line Cinema (and its specialty division, Fine Line Pictures) and Castle Rock (director Rob Reiner's company) became part of Turner Broadcasting along with Turner Pictures which in turn was absorbed by Warner Bros. Universal and Polygram (80 percent owned by Philips N.V.) formed Gramercy Pictures, which was so successful that Polygram Filmed Entertainment bought back Universal's share in 1995, only to be bought itself by Seagram-owned Universal. Eventually, Seagram sold October Films (one of the original indies), Gramercy Pictures and remaining PFE assets to Barry Diller's new USA Networks and those three names disappeared into history. Sony Pictures acquired Orion Classics, the only profitable segment of the original Orion Pictures, to form Sony Classics. Twentieth Century Fox formed Fox Searchlight, Fox 2000, and Fox Family Films. Metromedia, which owned Orion, bought The Samuel Goldwyn Company and eventually was bought itself by MGM. Not to be left out of the specialty film biz, Paramount launched Paramount Classics in 1998, and in August 2003 Warner Bros. formed a specialty film division, Warner Independent Pictures, headed by Mark Gill.

In 2003, Good Machine, a longtime producer and distributor of independent films became part of Universal as Focus Features. The partners split between going to Universal and staying independent as Good Machine International. It is unclear what the arrangements are between Universal and Focus; at this point, even I don't know if the produced films can be classified as independents. However, as with the other specialty divisions, the films that Focus acquires for distribution are independents. There is not room to go through a biography of all the independent companies, but their history is easily traced in the trade papers.

Then there is the debate about DreamWorks SKG. Formed in 1994 by Steven Spielberg, David Geffen, and Jeffrey Katzenberg, the company has variously been called a studio, an independent, and—my personal favorite—an independent studio. Capitalized at somewhere north of $2 billion, it is big. Yet, although it is in a class by itself, DreamWorks SKG is still an independent.

At one point, AOL Time Warner reportedly planned to sell New Line for $1 billion (Turner paid $600 million for the company in 1993) to reduce the parent company's debt load. New Line's founder, Robert Shaye, and the other principals had always made their own production decisions, even as part of Turner Pictures. In summer 1997, New Line secured a nonrecourse (i.e., parent company not responsible) $400 million loan through a consortium of foreign banks to provide self-sufficient production financing for New Line Cinema and Fine Line Features. Making their own films means that New Line keeps much more of their revenue than if they were a division of Warner Bros. Everyone liked this situation until the release of *The Lord of the Rings: Fellowship of the Ring*, the first film of the trilogy made for a reported total budget north of $300 million.

As part of an integrated company, specialty divisions have been able to give the studios the skill to acquire and distribute a different kind of film, while the studio is able to provide greater ancillary opportunities for the appropriate low-to-moderate budget films through their built-in distribution networks. If the films remain independently funded, the prime definition of being an "independent" has been met. It is up to you, the reader, to track what has happened in the meantime.

How It Works

An independent film goes through the same production process as a studio film, from development to postproduction. In this case, however, development and preproduction may involve only one or two people, and the entrepreneur, whether producer or director, maintains control over the final product. For the purposes of this discussion, we will assume that the entrepreneur at the helm of an independent film is the producer.

The independent producer is the manager of a small business enterprise. She must have business acumen for dealing with the investors, the money, and all the contracts involved during and after filming. The producer is totally responsible from inception to sale of the film; she must have enough personal power to win the confidence of the director, talent, agents, attorneys, distributors, and anyone else involved in the film's business dealings. There are a myriad of things the producer must concentrate on every day. Funding sources require regular financial reports, and production problems crop up on a daily basis, even with the best-laid plans. Traditionally, the fortunes of independent filmmakers have cycled up and down from year to year. For the past few years, they have been consistently up. In the late 1980s, with the success of such films as *Dirty Dancing* (made for under $5 million, it earned more than $100 million worldwide) and *Look Who's Talking* (made for less than $10 million, it earned more than $200 million), the studios tried to distribute small films. With minimum releasing budgets of $5 million, however, they didn't have the experience or patience to let a small film find its market. Studios eventually lost interest in producing small films, and individual filmmakers and small independent companies took back their territory.

In the early 1990s, *The Crying Game* and *Four Weddings and a Funeral* began a new era for the independent filmmaker and distributor. Many companies started with the success of a single film and its sequels. Carolco (which declared bankruptcy in 1996) built its reputation with the *Rambo* films, and New Line achieved prominence and clout with the *Nightmare on Elm Street* series.

Other companies have been built on the partnership of a single director and a producer (or group of production executives) who consistently create high-quality, money-making films. Imagine Entertainment (Ron Howard and Brian Grazer) and Castle Rock Entertainment (Rob Reiner and his four partners) are prime examples. These companies have gone through too many changes since their inception to track them all here—going public, establishing exclusive distribution deals with major studios, and sometimes even taking the studios in as investors. Imagine and Castle Rock have both taken steps to regain their creative and/or financial autonomy.

Then there are the smaller independent producers, from the individual making a first film to small or medium-sized companies that produce multiple films each year. The smaller production companies usually raise money for one film at a time, although they may have many projects in different phases of development. Many independent companies are owned or controlled by the creative person, such as a writer-director or writer-producer, in combination with a financial partner or group. These independents make low-budget pictures, usually in the $25,000 to $5 million range. *Clerks* and *The Brothers McMullen*—both made for $30,000 or less—are at the lower end of the range, often called "no-budget." When a film rises above the clouds, a small company is suddenly catapulted to star status. In 1999, *The Blair Witch Project* made Artisan Entertainment a force to contend with, and in 2002, *My Big Fat Greek Wedding* was a hit for IFC Films (recently sold by Rainbow Media to NBC as part of the Bravo Network) and brought Gold Circle Films into the ranks of small, independent distributors.

Tracking the Independent Dollar

Before trying to look at the independent film industry as a separate segment, it is helpful to have a general view of how the money flows. This information is probably the single most important factor that you will need to describe to potential investors. Wherever you insert this information in your plan, make sure that investors understand the basic flow of dollars from the revenue sources to the producer.

Table 4.2 shows where the money comes from and where it goes. The figures given are for a fictional film and do not reflect the results of any specific film. This simplified example provides an overview of how this works. In this discussion, the distributor is at the top of the "producer food chain," as all revenues come back to the distribution company first. The distributor's expenses ("P&A", or prints and ads) and fees (percentage of all revenue plus miscellaneous fees) come before the "total revenue to producer/ investor" line, which is the "net profit."

The boxoffice receipts for independent films are divided into exhibitor and distributor shares, just as they are for studio films (see Table 4.1). Here, however, the average split between distributor and exhibitor is 50/50. This is an average figure for the total, although on a weekly basis the split may differ. Generally, independent companies do not have the same clout as the studios, and the exhibitor retains a greater portion of the receipts. In the example, of the $9.00 million in total U.S. box office, the distributor receives $4.5 million in rentals. This $4.5 million from the U.S. theatrical rentals represents only a portion of the total revenues flowing back to the distributor. Other revenues are added to this sum as they flow in (generally over a period of two years).

The film production costs and distribution fees are paid out as the money flows in. From the first revenues, the prints and ads (known as the "first money out") are paid off. In this example, it is assumed that the P&A cost is covered by the distributor. Then, generally, the negative cost of the film is paid back to the investor. Often the investor will live with a 90/10 or 80/20 split with the producer until the initial investment is paid off. After the distributor has taken his fees (35 percent or less), the producer and the investor divide the remaining money.

TABLE 4.2
Tracking the Independent Dollar
($ Millions)

*REVENGE OF THE CRAZED CONSULTANT**	
Domestic Boxoffice Gross	9.0
Exhibitor Share of Box Office (50%)	4.5
Distributor Share of Box Office (50%)	4.5
REVENUE	
Domestic	
Theatrical Rentals (50% of total box office)	4.5
Television/Cable/Other	2.0
Video	5.0
	11.5
Foreign	
Theatrical	4.0
Television/Video	6.0
	10.0
TOTAL DISTRIBUTOR GROSS REVENUE	21.5
LESS:	
BUDGET	2.5
PRINTS AND ADVERTISING	5.5
TOTAL COSTS	8.0
GROSS INCOME	13.5
Distributor's Fees (35% of Gross Revenue)	7.5
NET PRODUCER/INVESTOR INCOME	
BEFORE TAXES	6.0

*This is a fictional film.

Pros and Cons

Independent filmmaking offers many advantages. The filmmaker has total control of the script and filming. Depending on agreements with distributors, it is usually the director's film to make and edit. Some filmmakers want to both direct and produce their movies; this is like working two 36-hour shifts within one 24-hour period. It is better to have a director direct and a producer produce, as this provides a system of checks and balances during production that approximates many of the pluses of the studio system. Nevertheless, the filmmaker is able to make these decisions for herself. And if she wants to distribute as well, preserving her cut and using her marketing plan, that is another option—not necessarily a good one, as distribution is a specialty in itself, but still an option.

The disadvantages in independent filmmaking are the corollary opposites of the studio advantages. Because there is no cast of characters to fall back on for advice, the producer must have experience or must find someone who does. Either you will be the producer and run your production, or you will have to hire a producer. Before you hire anyone, you should understand how movies are made and how the financing works. Whether risking $50,000 or $5 million, an investor wants to feel that your company is capable of safeguarding his money. Someone must have the knowledge and the authority to make a final decision. Even if the money comes out of the producer's or the director's own pocket, it is advisable to have the required technical and business knowledge before starting.

Money is hard to find. Budgets must be calculated as precisely as possible in the beginning, because independent investors do not have the same deep pockets as the studios. The breakdown of the script determines the budget. When you present a budget to an investor, you promise that you will keep the movie within the budget, and the investor agrees only on the specified amount of money. The producer has an obligation to the investor to make sure that the movie does not run over the budget.

PRODUCTION AND EXHIBITION FACTS AND FIGURES

The U.S. box office reached $9.5 billion in 2002, an increase of 13.2 percent over 2001 and the highest year-to-year increase in twenty years, according to the Motion Picture Association of America (MPAA). Worldwide sales for independent films in 2002 were more than $7 billion. Included in this number is a North American box office for indies of $3.4 billion and more than

$1 billion dollars in U.S. ancillary revenues as calculated by Business Strategies. Aggregate international sales (i.e., countries outside of the United States and Canada) for independent films are calculated by AFMA through a statistical survey of its members. Although the study for 2002 was not ready at press time, the AFMA survey showed total international sales in 2001 of $2.6 billion. While U.S. theatrical distribution is still the first choice of any feature-length film, international markets are gaining even greater strength than they had before.

Separating the gross dollars into studio and independent shares is another matter. While databases often include films distributed by specialty divisions of the studios as studio films, being acquired does not change the independent status of the film. In order to estimate the total for independent films, you have to add those from all the independent distributors plus films that have been acquired by Miramax, Sony Classics, and other distributing arms of the majors. As there is no database for "independent films acquired by studios," a precise figure is not possible.

Theatrical Exhibition

At the end of 2002, there were 35,280 theater screens (including drive-in screens) in the United States. This represents a decrease of 4 percent from 2001 and a decrease of 5 percent from the high of 37,396 screens in 2000. Since 1990, however, there has been an overall increase in the number of screens of almost 50 percent. The downward trend is attributed to the closing of run-down, out-of-date theaters that were competing with larger, state-of-the-art structures. Despite many ups and downs, such as the advent of television and the growth of the home video/DVD market, theatrical distribution has continued to prosper.

Film revenues from all other sources are driven by theatrical distribution. For pictures that skip the theatrical circuit and go directly into foreign markets, video, television, or another medium, revenues are not likely to be as high as those for films with a history of U.S. boxoffice revenues and promotion. The U.S. theatrical release of a film usually ends within the first year, many within the first three months. While studio films begin with a "wide" opening on thousands of screens, independent films start slower and build. The rentals will decline toward the end of an independent film's run, but they may very well increase during the first few months. It is not unusual for a smaller film to gain theaters as it becomes more popular.

Despite some common opinions from distributors, the exhibitor's basic desire is to see people sitting in the theater seats. There has been a lot of discussion about the strong-arm tactics that the major studios supposedly use to keep screens reserved for their use. (This is sometimes referred to as "block booking.") Exhibitors, however, have always maintained that they will show any film that they think their customers will pay to see. Depending on the location of the individual theater or the chain, local pressures or activities may play a part in the distributor's decision. Not all pictures are appropriate for all theaters.

Recent events have shown that independent films with good "buzz" (prerelease notices by reviewers, festival acclaim, and good public relations) and favorable word-of-mouth from audiences will not only survive but flourish. *Y tu mamá también* and *My Big Fat Greek Wedding* are the most recent examples. Both films started in a small number of theaters and cities. As audiences liked the films and told their friends about them, the movies were given wider release in chain theaters in more cities. Of course, good publicity gimmicks help. People still ask me if the 1999's *The Blair Witch Project* is a real story; I have even been accused of lying when I say that it is a fictional mockumentary!

Future Trends

Table 4.3 shows estimates of actual motion picture distributor revenue streams in 2001 and estimates for those revenues in 2010 forecasted by Kagan World Media as reported in the August 9, 2002 issue of "Motion Picture Investor" (see baseline.hollywood.com). According to the report, revenue was up, but the $1.4 billion gain was a growth of 4.5 percent compared to 6–7 percent growth in each of the prior four years and double-digit growth in the three years prior to that.

Overall, the next few years are looking good .... Not only has entertainment product been fairly recession-resistant domestically, but a much-stronger-than-expected 2002 domestic box office is expected to end the year with double-digit growth. This will drive up ancillary VHS/DVD sales as well as raise the value of the films in other windows, such as free and pay-TV.

Looking at Table 4.3, total distribution revenue is expected to grow 73.7 percent by 2010. Kagan World Media points out that

TABLE 4.3
Estimated Distributor Revenue Streams, 2001 and 2010
(Millions of Dollars)

	ACTUAL 2001	PROJECTED 2010
Revenue Source		
Domestic		
Theatrical Rentals	4,405	9,021
Home Video	8,270	12,317
Broadcast Networks	596	816
Syndicated Television	141	146
Pay Television	1,291	1,866
Basic Cable	1,420	2,469
Merchandising/Licensing	905	1,298
PPV/DBS/VOD	433	3,466
Hotel/Airlines/Other	70	119
Foreign		
Theatrical Rentals	3,279	5,536
Home Video	5,437	9,617
Network Television, Syndication	2,356	3,527
Pay Television	2,094	3,090
Merchandising/Licensing	1,591	2,420
PPV/Hotel/Airlines	122	596
TOTAL DISTRIBUTOR REVENUE	32,410	56,304

Source: Copyright © Kagan World Media, A Primedia Company. Used with permission.

by the end of the last decade, the theatrical box office dipped to 25 percent of worldwide revenues and dipped more to 23.8 percent in 2001. In 2010, however, worldwide theatrical revenues are expected to be almost 26 percent of the total. Although home video (VHS and DVD) will continue its growth (60% from 2001 to 2010), DVD will continue to get a larger piece of the home video pie until VHS becomes obsolete. By 2010, DVD sales and rental are forecasted at almost $30 billion compared to $11.5 billion in 2002. In comparison, VHS sales and rental will decline from $10.7 billion in

2002 to $76 million in 2010. The major change in film revenues is expected to come from technologies that have existed for several years but have not yet been a major factor—pay-per-view, direct broadcast satellite, and video-on-demand.

On the negative side, the international markets have not been taking as big a share of the total as previously expected. In 1999, the international revenues comprised 49.1 percent of the total revenue streams. In 2001, they comprised just 45.9 percent. Kagan World Media projects it to drop to 44 percent of total worldwide revenues by 2010. If that is true, the North American box office's influence in driving the rest of the revenue stream will continue to climb.

As you may be reading this book several years hence, be aware that the film industry is shifting at a greater rate than it ever did in the last decade. Many different and competing analyses and projections appear in the news media. A 500-channel television universe seems less certain than it did in the 1990s. Despite fears that the audience will leave the theaters and stay at home, most experts believe that theatrical exhibition will always be the vehicle that drives the popularity of products played in homes and in other outlets. People have always enjoyed an evening out and are expected to continue to do so. Even though you can watch a movie on your personal computer or send that signal to your home television, theatrical exhibition is not likely to disappear during our lifetime, and continues to flourish.

Digital Film

On June 5, 2000, Twentieth Century Fox became the first company to beam a movie over the Internet from a Hollywood studio to a theater across the country. Actually, it was to an audience at the Supercomm trade show in Atlanta after it had been sent from Burbank, California, over a secure Internet-based network. The film was the animated sci-fi epic *Titan A.E.* As we roll rapidly through the third year of the twenty-first century, filmmakers keep calling me about the $30,000 digital film they are going to make. But ask yourself a question: When will digital film be a business? My short answer is: When Regal Cinemas converts its more than 6,000 theater screens to digital projection. The company currently owns close to 20 percent of all the screens in the United States and is believed to have a long-term business strategy that is based on owning 30 percent.

How much progress have they made? Some movies have been digitally projected into select theaters. George Lucas put *Star Wars: Episode I—The Phantom Menace* in five theaters. Disney's *Dinosaur* was also shown digitally. However, while at this point it is important, digital film is not yet a business. A report by SRI Consulting at the time of our last printing stated that movies encoded as digital-data files "either recorded on optical disc and physically shipped or broadcast via satellite will increasingly replace film prints as the preferred method for distributing movies to theaters by 2005." With the release of *Star Wars: Episode II—Attack of the Clones* in May 2002, there were just 61 digital screens available worldwide to show the film, when it debuted in 3,000-plus theaters domestically. The film was still on screens in March 2003 with a domestic box-office to-date of $310.6 million. Anyone can do the math. That gross would not exist if the film had been released in digital format only. There is not a defnite count of digital screens in the world; however, by speaking to manufacturers, consultants have estimated that in the United States and Canada there are 80 d-cinema screens in 67 sites, with an additional 79 screens located in 75 sites internationally. At the ShoWest convention of exhibitors in March 2003, studio executives and equipment manufacturers stated their commitment to a digital future. At this point, however, there is no single accepted standard for equipment, and no one is volunteering to absorb the conversion costs, which are considerable. The cost for each digital projector is $150,000, along with the more than $20,000 per screen for the computer that stores and feeds the movies.

Until digital is bigger, if you choose to shoot in digital format, you must include money in your budget to upgrade your film to 35 mm. Don't assume that the distributor wants to do it. Look at it from his viewpoint. If the distributor is planning on releasing 10 to 20 films a year, at $55,000 or more per film for a quality upgrade, he is likely to opt for a film that is already in 35 mm format. "But," you say, "my film will be so overwhelming, he will offer to put up the money." It is within the realm of possibility, but I wouldn't want the distribution of my film to rest on that contingency. Or you may say, "I'll wait until the distributor wants the film, and then I'll raise the money for the upgrade." Although within the realm of possibility, don't assume just you will be able to raise the money. If you have formed an LLC, which is a favorite way for independents to raise money, and you go back to those people with another LLC for the $80,000, will they go for it? Maybe yes, maybe no. If they don't, then you are stuck.

Then there is the question of quality. When technology experts from the studios are on festival or market panels, they always point out that audiences don't care how you make the film; they care how it looks. If you can really make your ultra-low budget digital film have the look of a $5 million or $10 million film, go for it. But be honest with yourself.

WHAT DO YOU TELL INVESTORS?

All business plans should include a general explanation of the industry and how it works. No matter what your budget, investors need to know how both the studio and the independent sectors work. Your business plan should also assure investors that this is a healthy industry. You will find conflicting opinions; it is your choice what information to use. Whatever you tell the investor, be able to back it up with facts. As long as your rationale makes sense, your investor will feel secure that you know what you are talking about. That doesn't mean he will write the check, but at least he will trust you.

Tables and Graphs

A picture may be worth a thousand words, but 20 pictures are not necessarily worth 20,000. The introduction of user-friendly computer software has brought a new look to business plans. Unfortunately, many people have gone picture-crazy. They include tables and graphs where words might be better.

Graphs made up about three-fourths of one company's business plan that I saw. The graphs were very well done and to a certain extent did tell a story. The proposal, put together by an experienced consultant, was gorgeous and impressive—for what it was. But what was it? Imagine watching a silent film without the subtitles. You know what action is taking place, and you even have some vague idea of the story, but you don't know exactly who the characters are, what the plot is, or whether the resolution is a good one. Similarly, including a lot of graphs for the sake of making your proposal look nice has a point of diminishing returns.

There are certainly benefits to using tables and graphs, but there are no absolute rules about their use. Some of the rules for writing screenplays, however, do apply:

- Does this advance the plot?
- Is it gratuitous?
- Will the audience be able to follow it?

Ask yourself what relation your tables and graphs have to what investors need to know. For example, you could include a graph that shows the history of admissions per capita in the United States since 1950, but this might raise a red flag. Readers might suspect that you are trying to hide a lack of relevant research. You would only be fooling yourself. Investors looking for useful information will notice that it isn't there.

You will raise another red flag if you have multiple tables and graphs that are not accompanied by explanation. Graphic representations are not supposed to be self-explanatory; they are used to make the explanation more easily understood. There are two possible results: (1) the reader will be confused, or (2) the reader will think that you are confused. You might well be asked to explain your data. Won't that be exciting?

5

The Markets and Marketing

But the Devil whoops, as he whopped of old: It's clever but is it art?

RUDYARD KIPLING

You can take the 6.3 billion people in the world as a potential movie-going population, but very few filmmakers have expected to sell tickets to all of them—that is, until *Jurassic Park* pushed the boxoffice frontier farther than ever before in 1993. It earned more than $750 million worldwide. You didn't need to speak English or have to know anything about history to enjoy this film. It had something for everyone who was old enough to watch it. Then, in 1998, *Titanic* racked up $1.7 billion worldwide. More recently, both 2001's *Lord of the Rings: Fellowship of the Ring* and 2002's *Lord of the Rings: The Two Towers* have earned more than $800 million worldwide each. By the time you buy this book, the third film of the trilogy will be out. Check it's results.

What does this mean to you, the smaller independent? While studios are concentrating on very high budgets, there is no longer a ceiling for independents. This emphasis leaves a much larger part of the theatrical ballpark for the independent filmmaker making low-to-medium-budget movies. And the home runs being hit in the past five years have opened the game to many more players. In the mid-1990s, Steven Spielberg told *Premiere* magazine, "It's getting to the point where only two kinds of movies are being made—the tent-pole summer or Christmas movies or the sequels, and the audacious little Gramercy, Fine Line, or Miramax films.

It's like there's an upper class, a poverty class, and no middle class." More of the film middle class has now arrived.

In the last edition, I wrote about the financing of independent films by foreign companies and consortiums of investors and the growth in their numbers. In the past two years, many funds have failed; on the other hand, new companies and funds are aiming to take their place. Most of these money sources look for stars with an "A." Realistically though, your potential of having Tom Hanks star in your film is low. In fact, if you are a neophyte, it is probably a suicidal thought.

Whether your film is $400,000 or $40 million, has newbie actors or stars, you need to look at the market for your film. The market comprises those people who are going to buy tickets. We will be looking at the potential popularity of the themes and styles your films represent. To some extent, we also will look at marketing, but do not confuse these two concepts. Marketing involves selling your idea to the people who can help you get the film made. To make these terms somewhat more confusing, this book also refers to "the markets," such as the American Film Market and Cannes.

In the previous section of your business plan, you defined the industry as a whole and independent film as a segment of it. Now you will build on that definition by further dividing your industry segment. Your segment may not be as global in size as "everyone," but it has its own value. You will also take the products that you described in an earlier section and use their components to pinpoint your market. This analysis gives you a base for later estimating those very important ticket sales.

MARKET SEGMENT

Your market segment, or niche, is the people out of the total movie-going population that are likely to rush out to see your film the first weekend, as well as secondary target groups that will be interested. You need to identify, for yourself and those reading your proposal, the size and population characteristics of this segment. By devising a snapshot of your film's likely audience, you will be able to determine its ability, first, to survive and, second, to succeed. Who are the end-users of your film—that is, the ticket buyers—and how many of them are there likely to be? Before you worry about marketing strategies and distribution channels, create a picture of the potential size of your market's population. How can you do this? Very carefully. But do not worry. It is easier than you think; it just takes work. You do not need to have inside information or to live in Los Angeles to do this. Research is your tool.

Having divided the industry into parts, you now need to divide your segment into smaller pieces. In looking at this piece of the market, ask yourself these questions:

- How large a population segment is likely to see my film?
- What size budget is reasonable vis-á-vis the size of this segment?

Defining Your Segment

Filmmakers would like to appeal to everyone, and some mainstream films reach that goal. It is said that it is the big-budget action/adventure films that create the highest boxoffice grosses. This is true to a certain extent; the more money you spend, the bigger the audience you will attract—and the bigger the audience you will need to attract. An independent film, for the most part, will attract moviegoers from one or two identifiable segments of the audience. To understand how to focus your investor's expectations (and your own), you will have to do a little research. You do not have to be a research expert, but a little light investigation will help make you and your investor wiser and wealthier.

Creating a profile of your target market in terms of audience might include the following:

- Popular film genres
- Age
- Sex
- Personal preferences
- Successful budget parameters

To Pigeonhole or Not to Pigeonhole

Your identification of the target audience for your film begins when you select the genre of the film. The term "genre" can be very confusing. Some people appear to use the term to refer to cheap and formulaic, as in "it is a genre film." One client of mine was upset that I was cheapening her films by using the term "genre." For the business plans I write, it is used to refer to films that can be grouped together by plot, settings, and/or themes. Genre doesn't refer to how well you made the film or the amount of the budget. You could probably use the word "category," but it doesn't have the same feel.

As a genre, horror films, for example, are generally movies that scare you for some reason and have lots of blood and gore. Looking at the Internet Movie Database (imdb.com) for horror films, there are over 4,800 theatrical films listed ranging from the low-budget *Bloodsucking Killer Clowns from Outer Space* and *The Blair Witch Project* to the higher-budgeted *Lake Placid* and *The Sixth Sense*. The films have different premises (two deal with ghosts, two deal with blood and gore) and appeal to different audience segments. The over-40 group was more likely to be drawn to *The Sixth Sense* than anything with the word "bloodsucking" in the title and the initial target audience for that film. *The Blair Witch Project* was definitely a grabber for the 12 to 24-year-olds with repeat attendance a hallmark of that audience segment resulting in the film's high box office. In the end, though, both are still horror films.

Genres can be big or small. Drama is considered the most pervasive genre but is inclusive of almost every film that isn't a comedy. In second place in terms of number of films produced is usually comedy. Both of these genres include films that often carry descriptive adjectives, such as "family," "romantic," or "dark," to further narrow the category. Then we have thriller and action/adventure, both of which are dramas but different from one another. Defining the genre of a particular film can become unnecessarily complicated. In trying to be precise about identifying a film, the filmmaker may call it a drama/comedy/romance. This description covers all the bases. It fits *The Banger Sisters* which skewed to an older audience and *Shallow Hal*, which skewed younger.

There are also filmmakers who become their own genre. Saying a movie will be a Woody Allen film, a Robert Altman film, a John Waters film, or a Merchant-Ivory film creates a frame of reference for the particular experience moviegoers will have. These days, you can even have a producer genre. For example, a Joel Silver film would immediately be envisioned as another *Die Hard* 1–2, *Matrix* 1–3, or *Lethal Weapon* 1–4. This does not mean that his films will not fit into other genres, such as comedy. However, the filmmaker is so identified with a thriller type of experience that the audience will pick the film for the director rather than anything else. If you feel that your style is akin to a particular director's niche, you can draw from that audience.

Why bother identifying the genre for your film? Many writers and directors believe that categorizing their films is not only meaningless but in some cases demeaning. There are always filmmakers who say, "My picture is different and can't be compared to any other films." This entrepreneurial attitude is the same in all industries. All films can be compared, and you do have competition. By giving your investors these frames of reference, you are able to show the groups of moviegoers to whom the film might appeal and explain the genesis of your projections. One of the challenges you face with your business plan is being understood. You must be certain that you convey your meaning correctly to investors. It is important, therefore, that you define your terms so that everyone is on the same page.

Art versus Specialty

Over the last few years, I have participated in discussions on whether independent films are by definition "art" films and, if they are, what an art film is. In one such discussion, one person claimed that Federico Fellini and art films were one and the same. Someone else said that they "explain human foibles in an intellectual way." Another suggested that the term had nothing to do with subject.

In recent years, production and distribution companies have preferred the term "specialty" for their films rather than "arthouse," and with good reason. "Art" may bring to mind a very narrow vision of a type of film. Many would assume the film to be a boring, bogged-down film for the intellectually intense. "Specialty," on the other hand, is a broader term without these negative connotations. Until you define it, there may be no frame of reference for the investor. Creating a definitive description that everyone agrees with would be impossible. In writing your business plan, you have to find whatever phrases and film references best convey your meaning.

I have been involved with proposals for companies that intended to be like Miramax (a lot of people seem to want to be Miramax), Artisan, Lions Gate, or Sony Classics. What did we start with? We used those companies to define the genre. For example, you could write the following as your introduction:

> *We define the specialty market by the types of films acquired by Lions Gate Releasing and Sony Pictures Classics. Our films have a sensitivity of story and a delicate balance of characters that require unique handling. Therefore, our audience will be the same people who saw* Gods and Monsters, Monsters Ball *and* Real women Have Curves.

These pictures may have nothing in common in story or overall theme, but they are used to present a backdrop for the discussion; they give readers something to relate to. Of course, Lions Gate and Sony Classics do not have a lock on specialty films. Which companies you use for comparison depend on your feeling about their products and your reasons for making it.

An important aspect of specialty films is their distribution (and, consequently, revenue) potential. In recent years, the scope of specialty films has widened tremendously. Typically, a specialty film may open on 1 to 15 screens and expand to more screens as revenues become available. *You Can Count On Me* opened on 8 screens and slowly moved over three months to 39 screens. When its lead actress, Laura Linney, was nominated for a Best Actress Oscar, however, Paramount Classics jumped the number of screens to 139 the same week. On the other hand, if the distributor has enough money and faith, a small independent film can open on 100 or 200 screens the first weekend. *My Big Fat Greek Wedding* opened on 108 screens and, due to its extraordinary success, was on 2,014 screens at its widest distribution.

Genre History

When describing the history of a particular genre, you need not go back to Tom Mix or Gene Autry (ask your grandmother) for the Western genre. For the most part, your primary reference period should be the last five to six years. Some genres, such as action/adventure or comedy, are always going strong. They are always popular in one form or another. This is not the case with other genres, however.

Take horror again, for example. This genre, once popular, languished in the ultra-low-budget, direct-to-video/dvd, and direct-to-foreign world until the release of *Scream*. To that point, general wisdom was that horror films were not worth putting any money into; therefore, it was hard to get the investment community interested in the genre.

Timing is everything. Now money is available everywhere, not only for the traditional scary film (*The Mummy*, *The Mummy Returns*) but variations on a theme such as *Lake Placid* (comedy/horror) and *The Blair Witch Project* (mokumentary). Suppose you wanted to make a horror film before any of the above films were released. How would you have convinced someone that your film would be successful? There are several techniques you could use.

1. Emphasize other elements: *The Cell* is a thriller/horror in which a psychotherapist must race against time to explore the twisted mind of the killer to find where he has buried a woman.
2. Redefine the genre: *New Guy* is a comedy about a paper-pusher at a company whose motto is "Sacrifice Equals Success." After a long day of embarrassments, he is locked in the office overnight and finds the real meaning of the word "sacrifice."
3. Override the horror genre altogether: *The Sixth Sense* is a psychological thriller in which a child psychologist treats a disturbed young boy who thinks he sees ghosts. The film has a twist at the end that will bring interest from the potential audience in the same way as the "secret" in *The Crying Game*.
4. Use the cycle theory: *The Blair Witch Project* is a mockumentary/horror film. While neither of these genres have been financially successful in recent years, we believe that the filmmakers' fresh and original touches, such as the audience's uncertainty about whether the story is true or not, will create favorable word-of-mouth for the film and bring back these genres.

More about Cycles

The last technique is not a spurious argument. The popularity of a particular genre often rises and falls in cycles. For example, horror films, which made up 24 percent of the product at the 1989 American Film Market, were less than 3 percent of the total in 1993 and rose back to 6.3 percent by 2003. (Interestingly, the genre fell out of favor in the book industry at the same time.) Statistics like these, by the way, can be part of your extended discussion.

A successful film often inspires a number of similar films that try to capitalize on the popularity of the original. Film-noir—a term coined by French movie critics to describe American crime dramas in the 1940s—had a resurgence in the 1990s. After a brief reappearance of the genre in 1962 with the original *Cape Fear*, the genre's real resurgence began with Martin Scorsese's *Cape Fear* remake in 1991 followed by, among others, *The Usual Suspects* in 1994. It encouraged a proliferation of updated film-noirs (the darkly lit look of the forties films contributed to the term), such as Joel and Ethan Coen's *Fargo*, David Lynch's *Lost Highway*, Carl Franklin's *Devil in a Blue Dress*, Steven Soderbergh's *The Underneath*, Atom Egoyan's *Exotica*, Curtis Hanson's *L. A. Confidential* (won two 1997 Oscars for Best Supporting Actress and Adapted Screenplay and was nominated for six more, including Best Picture), Simon West's *The General's Daughter*, Phillip Noyce's *The Bone Collector*, and David Fincher's *Fight Club*. These films have broadened the boundaries of the genre beyond the detective thriller to represent a way of looking at the world through a dark mirror reflecting the shadowy underside of life. (Note that, being purists about the term "film-noir," the Internet Movie Database lists all the post-1950 films in this category as "neo-noir.")

Considering the length of time from development to release, the market may be glutted with a particular type of film for two or three years. When this happens, the audience may reach a saturation point and simply stop going to see films of that genre. Then someone comes along with a well-crafted film that makes money, and the cycle begins again.

Who Is Going to See This Film?

Do you know the age and sex of the person most likely to see your film? Market research properly belongs in the hands of the person doing the actual marketing (probably the distributor), but you can estimate the appeal of your potential market based on its age groups. For example, one animated film may be aimed primarily at children aged 12 and under. Another animated film, with a slightly more hip theme and a pop music soundtrack, may entertain children but also draw in teenagers and young adults. Disney's hit *Beauty and the Beast* was geared for and received the entire age population, from the very young to the very old, while Ralph Bakshi's X-rated animated film *Fritz the Cat* skewed to an older, very special niche audience.

Teen films are targeted toward an affluent and sizable group. Think *Bring It On, Dude, Were's My Car?*, and *10 Things I Hate About You*. Teenage movies are traditionally released at the beginning of the summer when schools are out and kids have a lot of time to go to the theater. And they often go to the same movie more than once.

Studios are particularly eager to make films for the teen and young adult market—usually defined as people between the ages of 12 and 24. Still, the single largest audience block, they made up 39 percent of moviegoers in 2002, according to the MPAA's "U.S. Economic Review 2002." The rest of the audience makeup is 11 percent ages 25–29, 18 percent 30–39, and 32 percent over 40. Unfortunately, the National Association of Theater Owners which collects this data for the MPAA does not count anyone under 12; therefore, the previous percents add to 100. Since family films have made big inroads, such data would be very helpful in explaining that segment to investors. These admissions measurements change from year to year; therefore, you will want to check the MPAA's Web site (mpaa.org) for current information.

Various independent distributors have planned their growth based on films with adult themes (not to be confused with porn). October Films (now part of USA Films), for example, never catered to the teen audience. Its cofounders were Bingham Ray, who heads MGM/UA's specialty division and Jeff Lipsky, co-founder of Lot 47, a distributor specializing in eclectic low-budget films such as *Scotland, PA, L.I.E.*, and *The War Room*.

Special Niche Groups

Certain groups of films initially appeal to a small segment of the population to start and then grow, often to the surprise of the filmmaker, to become a crossover film. *Y tu mamá también* is an example of a film in Spanish that initially was targeted to an older, Hispanic/Latino audience and attracted a significant number of "under 40" filmgoers. The high cost structures of the studios inhibit their ability to exploit smaller, underdeveloped markets, but independent filmmakers have the ability to take chances. They can make a low-budget or even a "no-budget" film to play to a tiny initial market. If the film and its theme catch on, the audience grows, and the film's genre crosses over to a larger portion of the public. Subsequent films of that type draw on the larger audience.

When the first edition of this book was published, it appeared to be big news that African-American filmmakers could draw an audience. Throughout the rest of the 1990s, gay and lesbian films came to the fore. At this vantage point in 2003 we have other niche audiences that producers and distributors have "discovered" go to the movies.

Until recently, The Walt Disney company seemed to have a lock on family films. It was almost impossible for independents to break into that category. Now Hollywood seems to have discovered that not R-rated films but G- and PG-rated are its next best thing. The industry made its biggest profits in 2001 from G- and PG-rated movies, according to a report in the *Los Angeles Times*, and plans to fill the nation's screens in the next few years with even more princesses, monsters, talking animals, bright school kids, and scrappy ballplayers. The independent film *My Dog Skip* was at the forefront of the family-film renaissance in 2000. This was followed by Dimension's *Spy Kids*, a breakout hit with a U.S. boxoffice of $113 million that inspired a sequel and a flock of imitators. Feeding the burgeoning family film market through 2002 are such films as *Spy Kids 2*, *Hey, Arnold*, and *Jonah: A Veggie Tales Movie*.

At the March 2002 Show West, an annual meeting of film exhibitors, John Fithian, President of the National Association of Theater Owners (NATO), said, "Part of the explanation for the success of 2001 comes from an important trend toward family-friendly films, a trend strongly supported by NATO. Year after year, the box office tells an important story for our friends in the creative community. Family-friendly films sell." He added that the five top films each grossed more than $200 million and none were rated "R"; and of the top 20 films, all of which grossed more than $100 million, only three were rated "R."

Faith-based (religious-themed, spiritual-themed, whatever you want to call it) films have also started to make an impact on the general film audience. The success of *The Omega Code* and *A Walk to Remember* are among several films that have alerted production companies and distributors that there was a market for inspirational films. One part of it, the Christian segment of the moviegoing public, has been estimated at 70 million people including all ages. In 1999 and 2000 both *Newsweek* and *Time* had cover stories about this market. What once was a video business supplied mostly by Christian booksellers has now become a part of the theatrical film experience. However, Ted Baehr points out in his book, *The Media-Wise Family* that in making a "good news" film, you still have to make a good film with entertainment value. Research indicates that the same percentage of Christian teenagers as non-Christian teenagers watch R-rated films with the same frequency. There is no reason why you can't make a film that reaches a large segment of the audience. My admonition to my faith-inspired filmmaker clients is to make a film that has a subtle message and doesn't announce an agenda to me. Samuel Goldwyn has often been quoted as saying, "If you want to send a message, call Western Union."

In the last two years, filmmakers also have been playing successfully to the Hispanic. (A Latino client has informed me that I may use the word "Hispanic" to describe the Hispanic/Latino market.) A relatively untapped group in terms of film marketing, Hispanics buy about 15% of all movie tickets. Fueled by fast population growth, a study by Global Insight predicts that by 2012 Hispanics will account for about 18% of ticket purchases, equivalent to about $2.9 billion in sales. The age profile of U.S. Hispanics skews younger than that for Anglos, 26 versus 32. These moviegoers are concentrated in the trend-setting major markets that make or break Hollywood releases. Until recently, it was hard for films by Latinos about Latinos to crack the codes of getting a distributor or attracting that specific audience.

The U.S. debuts in 2002 of two highly regarded movie imports from Latin America—*Y tu mamá también* and *El Crimen del Padre Amaro*—demonstrates how well ethnic films can perform both in their own regions and in the more lucrative U.S. market. They are part of a group of films that, along with other films from Mexico *Amores Perros*, and *The Son of the Bride*, and *City of God* from Brazil that have made the most impact. From U.S. filmmakers, *Frida*, *Real women Have Curves*, and *Tortilla Soup* have helped awaken the giant. Clearly, the films have more going for them than the facts that they are in Spanish or involve Hispanic or Latino casts. But they have the attention of the power brokers—investors and distributors. That is what counts.

The success of the films also is bringing more attention and investment to U.S. filmmakers who want to make films with Hispanic/Latino themes. "Every couple of years there is a different part of the world that's in the forefront of quality filmmaking,"

Michael Barker, co-president of Sony Pictures Classics told *Daily Variety*. "Latin America in the last couple of years has really risen." A further sign of the genre's strength is that Universal Pictures, which formed an exclusive arrangement with the Arenas group in 2001 to serve the U.S. Hispanic filmmakers and market, is moving to a multi-supplier arrangement. The change is "in recognition of the diversity, complexity and breadth of the opportunities provided by the Latino market," said Marc Shmuger, Vice Chairman of Universal Pictures.

Production Cost

When writing a business plan, you need to find as many ways to support your argument as possible. A valid comparison for films is the amount of the production (negative) cost. In some cases, the cost is additional confirmation for your assertions; in other instances, it may be your only argument. There are as many configurations of a film's budget as there are producers. No two situations are ever alike. So we will take the most common cases and let you extrapolate from there.

Case 1: Similar Films, Similar Budgets

Your films should be able to make the same or better revenues. When preparing your proposal, the first step is to read every interview with the filmmakers that you can find. You will usually be able to find information on how they made their pictures work—creating a production budget, finding a distributor, and getting by on a low budget. The market is more open for a small film to be successful than it has ever been. The potential for having a breakout film gets higher with the release of each successful film.

Case 2: Similar Films, Higher Budgets

If your film has a story or theme similar to that of others but will be made with a significantly higher budget, you can point out that better attachments are likely to help bring in more revenue.

If you have a well-known director who will draw some attention, be sure to mention that it is another Arthur Artiste picture. For a film with a budget of up to $1 or $2 million, both the director and the stars can be unknown; the film will rely totally on its story and quality. For a larger film, though, story and quality will still matter, but name value will mean even more.

Case 3: Different Films, Moderate Budgets

There may be a ceiling on the ability of niche films to grab the market. One strategy in this case is to start with moderate budgets that have mainstream potential. For this example, we will assume that you will start with a $5-million movie and move up to a much broader market. Always keep your genre in mind in addition to all the factors mentioned in Case 2.

There are many variations to putting together your comparative films and your explanations of the markets for your film. The point is that you should build on what exists. No matter what your niche market—and it may be a specialized one that has not really been explored yet—the same principles apply. Take the experience of similar films and use it to your advantage.

Even with these three cases, a discussion of the success of similarly budgeted films is in order. For example, in a business plan for gay/lesbian films, the producers planned to make three films over a five-year period with a budget of $500,000 for the first film, $2 million for the second, and $7 million for the third. Their argument was that the company would gain a reputation from the first film and would use that to grow on as the subject matter became part of a continually expanding market. Because there were no gay/lesbian films made with $7-million budgets to use for comparison, they created tables of other niche films with similar budgets.

Detailed tables showing the actual results of other films with similar budgets belong in the Financial section of your plan. Here, however, you can use the summary information to build a story. Gather comparative market information to prove the size and extent of the audience for your film.

What if you do not know the budgets of the films you are going to make? Your case will be much weaker, but you can still develop a rationale. Showing the results of films at various budgets will help. The other elements of your company, as described in Chapter 3, "The Projects/Products," can bring more credence to your proposal. If you have well-known directors or actors committed to your projects, you can use their previous films to describe a segment of the market.

MARKETING STRATEGY

Marketing strategy is usually defined as the techniques used to make the end-user aware of a product. In film, you have more than one potential end-user, more than one person who might queue up to the box office to buy a ticket. There is also an intermediate end-user, the money person. The ticket buyer will not read your business plan. Instead, your marketing is aimed at those who might provide the financing to make those ticket purchases possible. First, we'll look at your own strategies for getting the film made. Then, we'll look at some of the marketing tactics that distributors and producers may use for the film.

Experts often talk about the four Ps of marketing: product, price, place, and promotion. We have already touched on the first three in this section. In the Marketing section of your business plan, you don't want to forget promotion. Eventually, the distributor probably will be responsible for the specific tactics of fulfilling a marketing plan, but you can describe for investors what some of these tactics might be.

Market Research

As cognizant as investors or distributors might be about the emergence of a niche market, they may not know its true scope. Part of the promotion of your company is to obtain as much market research data as possible to bolster your contentions. In the normal course of finding financing for one film, this activity is helpful but not necessary. In putting together a company, however, you have different obligations and responsibilities. Gathering data on the feasibility of your concept is one of them. Part of that information is contained in your description of the market segment. However, you can go a step farther and get real facts and figures.

There are many formal and informal ways to gather information. Many of them are right in your own backyard. You can gain a lot of knowledge with a minimum of time and effort if you know how. Granted, some of these tricks of the trade are easier the closer you are to Hollywood or New York, but with the proliferation of events to which "Hollywoodites" travel and the proliferation of resources on the Internet, being from another city is not a good excuse for failing to do adequate research. Your task may be a little harder, but you can still accomplish it.

Reading—A Lost Art

The hardest idea to get across to many filmmakers is that they need to become voracious readers. Many creative folks are too busy doing their own thing to take time out to read. This is a big mistake. There is a lot of information available to you if you will take the time and trouble to find it. Even seasoned professionals say, "But I don't have time." The truth is that you cannot afford not to have time.

The primary source for people in the film business is the trade papers, primarily *The Hollywood Reporter* (hollywoodreporter.com), *Daily Variety* (variety.com), and a U.K. publication *Screen International* (screendaily.com). Those who are serious about having a business or even participating in the industry will do themselves a favor by subscribing to either the Net or print issue of at least one of the U.S. publications. Many people argue, "I can't afford it," but in the long run, it will be the cheapest way for you to get the most information. *Screendaily* sends out a daily e-mail and you can search their Website for free.

The trades have the news articles that tell you who is doing what with whom and how much it is going to cost. If you follow these sources carefully, you can pull out enough data to fill in the basic financials for any package. Nestled among the press releases and gossip are real facts on the production costs of many films and descriptions of how the producers found their financing. The reviews of new movies often make comparisons to similar films or discuss breakthrough pictures in terms of their genres. *The Full Monty* and *The Blair Witch Project* are examples of low-budget films that generated much comment in the media with last year's darling being *My Big Fat Greek Wedding*. At the height of that film's success, several small films that had hitherto languished without a release date suddenly found a distributor riding in on a white horse to send them out theatrically to enthusiastic reviewers.

The trades also publish lists of films in production, preproduction, and development. From the production columns, you can learn what genres of films are being made and with what types of casts. Some of the preproduction material is real and some is fantasy, but it gives you a fair idea of what people want to produce. You can list your films in the development columns free of charge. Many filmmakers have gotten contacts with production companies and distributors that way. Placing announcements also gives private investors a chance to hear about you. Many people with the ability to finance films choose to remain incognito; otherwise, they would be deluged with unwanted phone calls or scripts. They do read the trades, however, and it gives them the opportunity to contact producers whose stories interest them. Admittedly, this may be a long shot, but it does not cost you anything, and it gets your name out there. And if you see anything that looks just like your film, don't worry. You will make a better film!

One interesting quirk about Hollywood, and this is probably true of other places as well, is that people have more respect for names they recognize than for those that are unfamiliar. They will not necessarily remember where they saw or heard your name, but familiarity results in returned phone calls. Therefore, any opportunity to get your name in print is helpful.

Another benefit of reading the trades is that you learn who the movers and shakers are. Take the case of Robert Rodriguez, writer-director of the $7,000 miracle film, *El Mariachi*. He did not know any agents or others in Los Angeles, but he saw the name of Robert Newman, an agent at ICM (one of the three largest talent agencies in the entertainment business), in the trade papers and sent him the film as a sample director's reel. Newman took it to Columbia. Rodriguez went on to make *Spy Kids 1* and *2* (3 is currently in filming). Now people have to know his name!

Besides the industry publications, you can find a lot of information in regular monthly magazines that have no direct connection to the film industry. Let's look at just a small sampling of magazines. Interviews with producers or directors of independent films and articles with business statistics were published recently in such non-entertainment publications as the *New York Times*, *Vanity Fair*, *Time*, *Newsweek*, and *Forbes*. Local daily newspapers and *USA Today*, a national daily, also carry interviews in their entertainment and business sections. The proliferation of sites on the Internet has made this information far more accessible and, in many cases, free. The most useful of these, from my viewpoint, is the Internet Movie Database. Be alert; wherever you are, there is information available.

Networking

My first Sundance Film Festival was also my first entertainment industry event. Until then, I had worked in "real business," creating business plans and corporate strategies. Although I will admit to mixing and mingling at meetings before, I had never tried to "work a town." I knew no one and had a general feeling of nausea as I got off the plane. On the shuttle to Park City, everyone was silent. Finally, I asked a gentleman sitting behind me if it was his first trip. He and his friend turned out to be film commissioners. We chatted the rest of the way. That night I went with them to the opening night gathering and met more people. The next day, I chatted with those people and learned a lot about how they had financed their films and other salient information. Had I not spoken to the first two people, I might never have met the rest. The concept of networking this way can be very scary, but you can do it. Being friendly is not only a way to gather information, but also to make yourself known to others.

Why do you want to network? Your best sources of information may be going to seminars, luncheons, industry meetings, festivals, and markets. Besides listening to whatever public speaking occurs, you should go up and introduce yourself to the speakers, and you should mix with other people in the room.

There is no better source for information than other independent filmmakers. Whenever you have a chance to meet filmmakers, grill them for advice and facts. People like to talk about their experiences and, especially, their successes. (If this were not the case, I would not be able to get well-known filmmakers for my classes and seminars.) You will learn more from someone who has done what you are interested in than from all the books in the world.

Libraries and Computer Sources

Like reading, another lost art appears to be the ability to do research in a library. When teaching a course, I have been stunned to find out that graduate students have never heard of the Business Periodicals Index and other common library reference tools. Rumor has it that they still exist. If you are a student, take advantage. Although many computer sites have vanished since Edition 3 of this book, basic research ones are still there.

In writing a business plan, you must be concerned with more than just film grosses. You must be able to discuss the markets, the environment, ethnic groups, population figures, societal trends—whatever is pertinent to your projects and to your ticket buyers.

In addition, a business plan should contain specifics about other companies, industry mergers and acquisitions, new industries, and so on.

The first sources for this information are all those articles and books you never read or even knew existed. Besides visiting bookstores, go to your local library, a film-school library, or a general university library. If you live near Los Angeles, you have the added advantage of the library of the Academy of Motion Picture Arts and Sciences.

Look up your subject in the Business Periodicals Index and other periodical guides in the library. Many libraries have systems that allow you to do a computerized search of subjects. Finally, do not forget your friendly librarians; they are there to help you.

Through your computer, you can log onto the Internet and use online services to do library searches without ever leaving home. Mentioned previously are the Internet Movie Database (IMDB) (free) and baseline.hollywood.com (subscription). For searching who directed or produced what film, the locations, release dates etc., IMDB is fine. For data, however, it is worth the subscription to go to Baseline. It is the most credible database with worldwide revenues and budgets.

Promoting Yourself and Your Projects

We make our own opportunities, as every overnight success will tell you. By doing all that market research, you have prepared yourself for two things:

- Quantifying your market segment
- Approaching others with your project

At the beginning of this chapter, we talked about the market segment; how it is time to focus on marketing yourself and your project. As noted before, your goal is to find the money or links to the money. There are entire books that focus on this subject, so I am providing you with just the basic information.

Arm Yourself with Ammunition

As a good promoter, there are certain materials you can prepare before seeking out contacts. Business cards, sales sheets, press kits, and director's reels are among the promotional materials you might use. Some filmmakers have even made a 45-minute version of the film itself, often on videotape, for promotion. For first-time filmmakers with no other footage to show, putting a long treatment on film may be the way to go.

More Networking

The materials just described serve to get you into meetings. Whether your aim is to sell a single film or to obtain financing for your company's group of films, the first step is to evoke interest. Making contacts is your objective, wherever you are. Earlier we talked about networking as a means of gathering information. Another purpose is to unearth those money sources, wherever they are.

People with like interests tend to congregate in the same places; therefore, entertainment-related gatherings are your most likely place for success. Although potential investors are not likely to be in attendance, their friends and acquaintances may be. Festivals and markets are critical for whatever you are selling, and working them is of the utmost importance. You do not want to be carrying around business plans, handing them to everyone who says, "I can get you a deal." That is why you bother with the materials described earlier. Those are the items you hand to people initially. Common sense will stand you in good stead in attending markets and festivals. There is no trick to meeting and greeting, no secret hand-shakes or passwords. When you attend a market, remember that a distributor's goal in being there is not to meet you; it is to sell product. Here are guidelines for you to follow:

- Be prepared: Bring your short-term promotional materials, and bone up on who is who before you go. Let your fingers do some walking through the trades.
- Be aware: Distribution companies usually focus on certain types of films. Look at their posters and at the items listed in their market catalogs. Try to match your films to their inventory. After all, the distributor is your shortest route to those foreign buyers and presales.
- Be inquisitive: Ask questions of everyone you meet—in an office, in the lobby, on the street. Try to discover the person's qualifications before spilling your guts about your plans and projects, however.

- Be considerate: In introducing yourself to distributors, pick slack times. Very early in the day and at the end of the day are best. Whenever you reach a distributor's display room, notice if buyers are there. If they are, go back later.
- Be succinct: Keep discussion short and sweet. Your objective is to get a meeting at a later time. You want your prey to feel relaxed and be attentive. Try for a meeting at the distributor's office.
- Be dubious: Lots of people are milling around towns and lobbies pretending to be something they are not. It may be a big rush for someone to tell you that they were the "real" investor behind *My Big Fat Greek Wedding* (when they had nothing to do with it) and are interested in financing your film for $2 million (when they have no money). Listen carefully, take cards, and try to verify the facts afterward. Do not give your scripts or proposals to anyone unless you can validate their credentials.

Distribution

6

"We don't think of ourselves as arthouses. We're street fighters for signature films."

DAVID LINDE
co-president Focus Features

Long before Carl Laemmle produced his first maverick film, middle-men existed (as did agents, attorneys, and litigation). These intermediaries bought low and sold high even then. Among the most maligned of all entrepreneurs, middlemen are still harshly criticized for doing their job.

Motion picture distributors are middlemen, and they are a curious lot. They are viewed either as people of tremendous skill nourishing the growth of business or as flimflam artists reaping obscene profits. Like politicians, distributors are sometimes seen as a necessary evil. They perform an important function, however, without which many businesses, and certainly filmmakers, would not thrive.

When writing your business plan, you will need to explain the distribution system. As with other elements of the plan, you should proceed on the assumption that your reader does not know how the system works. Wrong assumptions on either side could block the progress of your films and your company.

This chapter looks at distribution strategies in general, glances briefly at studio distribution, and examines independent distribution in some depth.

WHAT IS A DISTRIBUTOR?

History does not tell us when the term "distributor" began to be used. If you look through any other business plan book, chances are you will not see a category for distribution. Examine the table of contents and browse through the index; distributors are not there. All industries have wholesalers, but their role is more narrowly defined than in the film world. Elsewhere, wholesalers are customers for the manufacturer. They buy inventory product at discount prices, add a price markup, and resell at the higher price. In this sense, these intermediaries are considered just another one of the channels for getting the product to the market. They are not involved in making artistic decisions about the product, changing the name for better marketing, or obtaining premanufacturing financing.

Distributors have tremendous power, and in independent film, their impact is magnified. Studios normally have committees and different levels of people making a decision. In an independent distribution company, one person, with no one to answer to, may determine the entire course of your film. The distributor has the ability to influence script changes, casting decisions, final edits, and marketing strategies; in addition, distributors often are intimately involved in the financing of the film.

They have this power by virtue of the distribution agreement. The specifics of the distribution deal and the timing of all money disbursements depend on the agreement that is finally negotiated. As a new filmmaker, you have no leverage for changing this agreement. Even an experienced filmmaker seldom can exact any substantive changes in the standard contract. One can debate fee rates or credits. In the end, however, even though each deal is different, the basic contents stay the same.

Before the audience can buy a ticket or rent a video, the movie has to get off the producer's desk and into the movie theaters. This method of circulation is called distribution. Simply put, it is the business of selling the film to various media, such as theatrical, cable, video, DVD, pay-per-view, television, and nontheatrical (army bases, airplanes, ships at sea, and so on). But it is not simply done. The distributor must be a salesperson, an entrepreneur, a skillful negotiator and a raconteur, and must have a sixth sense about matching the buyer with the product.

The "rights" of a film stem from the ownership of the copyright, which endows the legal use of the film on the copyright holder. Having secured a formal copyright, the producer contractually licenses, or rents, the film to a distributor for a specific length of time. The producer can relinquish all control of the film by shifting the entire copyright to the distributor in perpetuity, or she can license a specific right, such as domestic, foreign, video, DVD, cable, television, satellite, PDA or cell phone to the distributor for a specific length of time. In return, the distributor collects the rental monies or ancillary fees and remits the producer's share.

The following is from our sample domestic distribution contract. Although it is a boilerplate (the starting point for negotiations), the following section is not likely to change:

> The "Rights" consist of the sole and exclusive right, license and privilege under copyright (including all extended and renewal terms thereof) to distribute, exhibit, market, reissue, advertise, publicize and otherwise exploit the Picture and the literary material upon which they are based, the picture, sound, music and all other physical elements thereof, and trailers in any and all media and by any and all means (whether now known or hereafter developed, discovered, invented or created) throughout the Territory ...

Armed with the rights, distributors go about the business of relicensing the film to the various media. The U.S. theatrical box office is the backbone in the chain of revenues for any film. All ancillary results are driven by the domestic theatrical release. Some products are made to skip that step and go directly to video, DVD, or foreign markets, but the value of a film in any other media and territories is generally greater with a good theatrical release. Even a small theatrical release can increase the value to buyers of an otherwise unknown film.

STUDIO DISTRIBUTION

How It Works

The major studios (and the larger production companies) each have their own distribution divisions. They not only release their own films, but occasionally acquire other films as well. All the marketing and other distribution decisions are made in-house.

The division sends out promotional and advertising materials, arranges screenings of films, and makes deals with domestic and foreign distributors. Because of their size and the quantity of completed films each year, the studios naturally have a lot of clout in getting their films onto theater screens.

For the foreign markets, studios have offices around the world, either singly or with other studios, to distribute their films in other countries. Often, a studio will partner with a local distributor, and the release will bear the names of both companies. The studio always retains the copyright, which it licenses to the foreign distributor for a specific length of time.

Based on the share formulas we saw in Chapter 4, "The Industry," the studio's distribution arm receives its share of the boxoffice grosses from the exhibitor and passes them through the accounting system. The studio charges distribution fees back against the film as if its distribution division were a separate company. These fees can range from 30 to 40 percent of the total film rentals. In addition, the studio takes the entire fixed cost of the distribution division (overhead) and applies a portion of it to each film. A studio's total share of the revenue can be 55 percent or greater.

Overhead fees pay for running the division and cover expenses that are not covered by other fees. Before the accounting day is done, the studio will also take a portion of the overhead from the production side of the studio and add it to the total cost of the film. The formula in Table 4.1 shows a "net profit" model for a studio film. Each studio has a standard method in its contracts for determining revenues, expenses, and profits. These formulas are nearly impossible to change, even by influential filmmakers. Typically, the producer has a percentage of the net profits in addition to receiving a salary. With studio films, it is fair to say that the chances of the net profit being greater than zero is rarer than with independent films. The studios have more films to cross-collateralize (using the profits from one film to offset the losses from another) and more places to bury unreasonable cost, although many contracts now prohibit films from being cross-collateralized.

The Advantages

There are many advantages to studio distribution. The studio has the ability to put 3,000 plus prints of one film in circulation on opening weekend. Its own channels of distribution are manifold. The studio has the financial resources to inundate television and the press with ads, and it has significant clout in getting placements for producers, directors, and actors on early-morning and late-night national interview shows. It may own television networks, both free and cable, assuring the downline distribution. On the other hand, the upside for the studio is being able to negotiate a deal with its own affiliate at a value on paper that is less than free market value.

As noted earlier, the studios have been able to monopolize the chain movie theaters in the past. Some have moved back into theater ownership. Be that as it may, with the success of independent films, exhibitors insist that they do not bow to studio pressure. They can only afford to have films in their houses that fill the theater seats. If the audience does not come to see a particular film, the exhibitor must look for another that will be more popular. With the success of independent films, exhibitors have made more screens available to them. Over the past decade, as small films have received acclaim, they have gone wide (in this case, 700 to 1,200 theaters) to major chains that would not have played them previously.

INDEPENDENT DISTRIBUTION

The Players, They Are A-Changin'

Ten years ago, neither this author nor Bob Dylan could have foreseen what would be going on now. Even though the first edition of this book said that it wasn't true, many would-be seers thought the independents would disappear. The intervening years have shown a total change in which studios have become more like independents. The Majors have acquired independent companies as the quickest way into the lower-budget market, and new independent companies continually have been formed to replace those that merged with other independents or became specialty divisions of studios. And, as happens with all editions of this book, as we go to press several companies are in play.

Companies that were new or expanding in the late 1990s have become more highly capitalized or have disappeared into new entities. Artisan Entertainment is a good example. At the same time that they were buying October Films in 1997, a consortium headed by investment firms Bain Capital and Richland, Gordon and Company bought Live Entertainment, which had one of the largest independent film libraries (2,000 titles) in the world, for $93 million. The new company became Artisan Entertainment. Then, Boston-based Audax Group bought a controlling share. In addition, today the company's other principal shareholders include investor Al Gordon of Richland, Gordon & Co. who owns about 15 percent and Ivan Fecan, president and CEO of Bell Globemedia, who owns 20 percent. Several executives played musical chairs from Miramax to October to Live after the two acquisitions. Artisan slowly built until 1999, when the success of *The Blair Witch Project* single-handedly moved the company into the front ranks of independent distribution. The story doesn't end there.

At that time, Bain was interested in purchasing Trimark Pictures, which began in 1990 as the motion picture arm of onetime video major Vidmark, but the sale did not happen. Meanwhile, an investor purchased Cinepix Film Properties and changed the name to Lions Gate Films. Two of the company's most successful films have been *Dogma* and *Gods and Monsters*. In 2000, Lions Gate bought Trimark Pictures for approximately $50 million. Currently, Artisan's investors are fielding bids to buy the firm. Among the known potential buyers are Marvel Entertainment and a group led by film producer Stanley Jaffe and former USA Film executive Scott Greenstein. Lions Gate made an early offer for the company that was turned down for being too low; however, they could rejoin the bidding. Did someone say independent distributors were dead? They did, but they were wrong.

Why do you care about all this financial machinations? First of all, you should know the history and personnel of the company with which you want to do business. How have they acted in the past, are they likely to be dealmakers who are more interested in selling the company for a profit than distributors for your film, or are they hands-on film lovers who are likely to be around for the long haul. Just the length of time that a company takes to negotiate a merger or buyout can hurt any film in its library. My favorite film from Sundance 2000, *Songcatcher*, was acquired by Trimark. By the time the Lions Gate/Trimark merger was complete, the film was in the library of the new company that may not have had the same regard for its potential success as the original buyers. The resulting release in June of 2001 may have been too late from the film's

Sundance Special Jury Award for Ensemble Cast to be meaningful. The new company appeared not to have put a lot of effort behind the release.

There's more. Also in the late '90s, Universal Pictures sold its 50 percent interest in Gramercy Pictures to its partner Polygram and bought a majority interest in October Films, an independent giving more credence to artistic merit than bottom line. The latter company had released its first film, *Life Is Sweet*, in 1991. By 1993, the company had completed a private placement, taken in other equity partners (one of whom, Amir Malin, was later a partner with Bain in buying Live), and expanded its ability to market and exploit its films. In 1998, Universal bought Polygram Entertainment and, in 1999, sold Gramercy Pictures and October Films to Barry Diller's newly formed USA Films. Those companies disappeared into the new parent. Jeff Lipsky, a cofounder of October, cofounded Lot 47 with his brothers Mark and Scott. Bingham Ray, the other cofounder, heads United Artists as the specialty division of MGM.

This acquisition/merger mania only gives credence to the good health of the independent group as a whole. As mentioned in Chapter 4, current specialty divisions of studios are Sony Classics, Paramount Classics, Focus Features, United Artists, and Fox Searchlight, with some form of a division at Warner Bros. likely. Miramax is Disney's specialty arm but has its own bank account and distribution division, seldom using Buena Vista. The other larger production/distribution companies are Lions Gate and Artisan. A few of the totally independent and smaller are First Look Pictures, Strand, Cowboy, IFC Films, Newmarket Films, Gold Circle Films, Manhattan Pictures, IDP Distribution, and Eros. I should put the date (May 2003) on the list, as it will change.

Do your own research to see who is doing what. Since the landscape is constantly changing in this dynamic industry, the independent filmmaker must function in a fluid environment. The small independent of today could be the Miramax of tomorrow.

How It Works

Watching the independent distributor at work takes in all the possible roles performed by the distributor. More than just a functionary for getting your picture out, the independent distributor can perform one or more other roles, including participating in creative decisions and contributing to the film's financial resources. For most independent filmmakers, the independent distributor is the only game in town and deserves an extensive look.

Domestic versus Foreign

The domestic territory generally comprises just the United States, but it might also be considered to include Canada and, many times, Puerto Rico, and other Caribbean islands. Many of the independent distributors consider the United States and Canada to be one North American package and prefer not to have them separated beforehand. For one thing, the distributor may have output deals with Canada. If the opportunity for Canadian financing arises, therefore, producers must be careful. If the Canadian investors are going to take some or all of the Canadian territory for themselves, the producer might have a problem finding a distributor for the U.S. market. Before signing such an agreement, therefore, it is best to find a distributor willing to take the United States.

Domestic rights refer not only to theatrical distribution but to all the other media such as video, DVD, cable, and the Internet. A producer who secures an advance from one of these media for production financing makes the deal a little less attractive to the distributor, because the rights have been fractionalized, or split up. Any source of future revenue taken out of the potential money pie before a distributor is found makes an eventual distribution deal tougher for the producer to close. Most distributors make a substantial investment in print and advertising costs. Although they may recoup these amounts from the theatrical marketplace, it is not likely to cover their distribution fees. Therefore, they prefer that other revenue sources be available to them.

A special word about Internet rights. Movielink is a company that was formed to sell downloadable digital copies of features, both first-run and library films. It is backed by Sony, MGM, Warner Bros., Universal, and Paramount, and has deals with Artisan, and some foreign film providers. Likewise, CinemaNow provides downloadable films on its website from more than 100 licensors including Warner Bros., MGM, Lions Gate Entertainment, Lot 47, Vanguard Cinema, and Visionbox Media. How big this Internet business will become is still unknown. There are other companies that will let you upload your film for free. What you have to know is that you do not want to license your film to anyone on the

Internet before you have a contract with traditional domestic and international distributors. Whether or not they will do anything with those rights, the distributors want them available. You will see in Chapter 11 that this is particularly crucial for short films.

Being a domestic distributor usually means that a company does not sell foreign rights themselves. Miramax started as a domestic distributor. The company's purchase of *Shall We Dance*, for example, involved only domestic distribution. Strand Releasing, Fine Line (specialty division of New Line), First Look Pictures (domestic division of foreign sales company Overseas Filmgroup), Manhattan Pictures, New Yorker, and IFC Films are other examples of domestic distributors. However, no rule says that a domestic distributor cannot venture into foreign waters. When Miramax lost its bid to distribute *Shine* in the United States, it picked up the foreign rights. In addition, any company will probably be willing to be a one-stop shop for you. For example, a domestic distributor can certainly arrange a deal for you with a foreign sales distributor, and vice versa. On the other hand, keep in mind that the more participants in a deal, the more fees are subtracted from it.

There also are U.S.-based distributors that specialize in foreign only. These companies deal with networks of subdistributors all around the world. It is sometimes confusing for producers to distinguish between a distributor and a foreign sales agent. If a distribution company is granted the rights to the film for the foreign markets, that company, whether it is one person or twenty, is the distributor. The company may be referred to as a foreign sales agent, also. There is no fundamental difference, just one of semantics. *The Hollywood Distributors Directory* is a good reference for both domestic and foreign distributors. Also, AFMA publishes an annual directory of their members.

Generally, the producer retains ownership of the copyright and only grants someone a percentage of the receipts for obtaining distribution contracts for a particular territory and/or medium. A typical term for granted rights is seven years, although some distributors will want ten.

A Deal Is a Deal

What is a typical deal? There is no such animal; no two deals are ever exactly the same. Distributors will take as much as they can get, and it is the producer's job to give away as little as possible.

Do not under any circumstances enter into one of these agreements without the advice of an entertainment attorney experienced in film. Some distributors will try to get you to sign an agreement before their fees are specified or without any agreement for theatrical distribution. Their business is to be persuasive, and they are good at it. The attorney knows what needs to be in the agreement before you sign it. He can be equally persuasive.

The attorney's film experience is important. When I was first advising filmmakers, I would tell them to get an entertainment attorney. Sometimes they would find someone who worked in music or with stage productions. Film is a specialty, and you want your attorney to be familiar with it. The other mistake that filmmakers often make is using their father's corporate attorney to negotiate their film contract. The filmmaker ends up paying for the attorney's learning curve (lawyers charge by the hour), and, worst case, end up with a bad deal.

The distributor's fees vary from territory to territory or medium. This amount can be as low as 15 percent (for a "hired gun") or as high as 50 percent of the revenues from the film. Although most contracts treat domestic and foreign revenues separately, general wisdom says that the overall averages for a distributor's fees is 35 percent or under. If the contract calls for more money than that, you probably don't want to sign.

How much the distributor wants to take depends on the company's participation in the entire film package. The distributor may:

- Get a finished picture
- Provide print and advertising (P&A) money
- Be rented
- Raise equity or presale financing
- Provide a minimum guarantee
- Pay an advance

There are no hard and fast rules. A lot depends on how much risk the distributor is taking, whether or not she put in production money, and how badly the company wants the film. The amount of risk is primarily related to the amount of money the distribution company pays out of its pocket. The more upfront expenses it has to assume, the greater the percentage of incoming revenues it will seek. These percentages apply only to the revenues generated by the distributor's own deals; if that company is only making foreign sales for you, then it takes a percentage of foreign revenues only.

Do not assume knowledge about another film's agreement and promise the same deal to your investor. Often clients want me to give examples of purchase prices in their business plans. For example, the trades said that Miramax picked up the rights to *Happy, Texas* at Sundance 1999 for $10 million. But only one report stated that the total amount was tied to the total domestic box office. In reality, the producers received less than $3 million up front as an advance against future box office; it was not an outright purchase. It is unlikely that the producers and investors saw the rest of the money, as the $2.5 million film grossed less than $3 million in North America. Haxan Films, who made *The Blair Witch Project*, also made a deal that depended on an escalating box office. But they fared much better. The production company received $1.2 million as an advance against future box office and their eventual share of the blockbuster U.S. box office was $45 million. After payments to attorneys, investors, and others, the five members of the production team kept $20 million. You can use this as a hook to your investors, but you must make it clear that this is an anomaly and may never happen again, especially for a film that cost below $500,000 to make.

Sometimes a producer or director will give useful financial details in an interview. For example, Miramax paid $5 million for *Swingers* ($250,000 budget). According to director Doug Liman, who gave several in-depth interviews, approximately $750,000 of that amount paid off deferments and $1 million was paid in commissions to agencies, leaving an apparent $3 million for the producers and equity investors. Here is a good reason for that online subscription you bought for one of the trade papers. Look for the distribution history of *My Big Fat Greek Wedding*. Put it in your Internet search engine and see what happens. If you enter "The Blair Witch Project," eventually a *Forbes* article containing the data that I gave you in the previous paragraph will show up. Now you didn't think I would release a client's proprietary information, did you?

Prints and Ads Money

The first step in distributing a film is making copies of it. Prints are copies made from the master, which is made from the original edited negative. For all intents and purposes, the print is the specific motion picture release, as the master does not circulate. (It is kept in a vault for safekeeping and used when additional prints are necessary.) One print usually costs $1,200 to $1,500, depending on the length of the film and current film stock costs. A wide distribution can cost well over $3 million for prints alone. Independent distributors, who have much smaller budgets than studios, usually start with only a few prints—sometimes even one.

Many distributors encourage producers to provide the P&A money, because this limits their risk even more. Producers who do provide the P&A can negotiate a lower distribution fee, often ranging from 10 to 22.5 percent, with the most common fees being 15 to 17.5 percent. These deals—often called "rent-a-distributor" or "hired gun"—usually have an escalator clause to give the distributor an incentive. For example, the fee might be 15 percent until net revenues to the producer equal the cost of the film or some multiple of the cost of the film, at which time the distribution fees escalate to 17.5 percent. On the other hand, some distributors just negotiate a flat fee for working this way.

There are varied opinions on whether it is practical for a producer to pay P&A costs. By putting up the money, the producer lessens the amount that the distributor will receive from the total revenues. On the other hand, many believe that the greater the distributor's share of the incoming revenues, the harder the company will work to maximize them. The producer may also be cast in the role of monitoring the value of the distribution process; without experience, how will you be able to judge? How to handle the P&A questions is one issue you have to decide for yourself. In the end, however, having to ask an investor for several million dollars in addition to the production costs may help you decide to forego this choice.

Distributor as Financier

Chapter 9, "Financing," discusses financing in detail, but let's look here at the situation that arises when the distribution company is the provider of funds. If the distribution company produces a minimum guarantee, it is taking on greater risk, and therefore the fees are higher. Sometimes, the deal may give the distributor an equity participation in the film on the back end. The distribution fee is taken off the top, expense reimbursements are second, and then the revenues are split on some percentage basis. The distributor is now on the hook for providing a minimum amount of money no matter what the film does. If the company has provided a bankable guarantee for the producer, the distributor has to make good on the bank loan.

DISTRIBUTOR STRATEGIES

The marketing of the film to the general public is the distributor's job. He makes decisions regarding the representation of the film in terms of genre, the placement of advertisements in various media, the sales approach for exhibitors and foreign buyers, and the "hype" (word-of-mouth, promotional events, alliances with special interest groups, and so on)—all of which are critical to a film's success.

Because marketing is part of the distribution company's area of expertise, it usually is unwilling to give the filmmaker a say in the sales strategy, the poster design, or how the film is portrayed. This comes as a shock to many filmmakers, who assume that they are going to have significant input or even a vote on how the posters look and where the film is opened. Many producers and directors expect a studio to ignore them, but they are under the impression that small distributors run their businesses as cooperative ventures.

Look at this from the distributor's point of view. Too many people involved in the decision-making process could be a nightmare. Formulating a marketing plan by committee could result in the proverbial camel. Artistic people tend to feel that they know the best way to present their project. After all, it is their baby, and they know it more intimately than anyone else. And how hard could advertising really be?

Franklin Delano Roosevelt said, "If I were starting life all over again, I would go into the advertising business; it has risen with ever-growing rapidity to the dignity of an art." We are all specialists, and marketing is the forte of the distributor. The filmmaker's task is to check out the distributor by researching other films the company has sold and the methods they used in the process. It is hoped that the distributor and the filmmaker will meet each other's standards and that a marriage will be made. Doing your own research to find the best distributor for you should head off a divorce later down the line.

What the Distributor Looks For

In acquiring a project, the distributor looks at many of the same elements discussed in Chapter 3, "The Films/Products":

- Uniqueness of story line
- Genre
- Ability of the cast members to attract audiences or buyers on their names alone
- Past successes of the producers or director
- Name tie-in from another medium, such as a best-selling novel
- Special audience segment for the type, or genre, of film
- Attached money

Being able to sell a film involves a mix of elements, although the story is always the first concern. The people to whom the distributors sell must see something in the film that will appeal to their audiences. This varies from country to country and depends on the perspective of the buyer.

No two buyers necessarily think the same. It is difficult to define why one distributor will buy a particular film,while the distributor in the next room at AFM will not. It often boils down to a gut feeling—a notion that the distributor knows how to sell and profit from the movie. Every company operates in its own particular niche, but on any given day some distributors are likely to find your film appealing.

As a producer, you cannot count on miracles or on someone's gut feelings, however. Your best bet is to make your product and your approach as strong as possible. The more components that you bring to the table with the film, the more ammunition your distributor has. Negotiating is their business, but they need something to bargain with.

To complicate your life even more, the definition of a saleable commodity can change from year to year or from market to market. While distributors are in the thick of the battle getting the latest information, the rest of us might be a year behind. This situation makes meeting and talking to distributors crucial. One year, when I was first in the business, I arrived at the American Film Market with a client to promote his already finished film. The director had convinced a well-known actress to do a 15-minute wraparound (inserting a well-known person into the film purely to make it more saleable). She had been popular at previous markets. Unfortunately, the most recent European market had seen a glut of films with this person, and when we arrived at AFM to make our pitch, there were yawns all around. The distributors knew she was old news, because it is their business. We had not thought to check beforehand to see if the star's popularity had changed.

Presales are another area that filmmakers often assume (and include in their business plans) as a given. However, you cannot count on such a sale until the deal has been completed. For example, when a film called *The Soldier's Wife* appeared at the 1992 AFM looking for presales, it already had experienced elements attached. Each of these elements was known in some markets, but not all; the American population was not familiar with the British stars (this was before Miramax's advertising blitz for the completed film). In addition, no one wanted to take a chance on the script at that time. When the film was eventually made and released, those elements were still attached, and the title was changed to *The Crying Game*. At what point the "secret" was included is not clear. Eventually, a consortium of British Screen Finance, Nippon Film Development, and Channel Four (from Britain) provided the financing. After Miramax's inventive publicity, the rest of the world had to see it to believe it.

Approaching a distribution company with a finished film has advantages. The distributor knows what you can do, and how it will look on the screen. The company's risk level is lowered, and its financial output is less. A finished film also puts you in a stronger negotiating position. Many distributors say that they prefer even partially completed films to scripts because they feel that there is less chance of being sued for stealing someone else's film.

Festivals are another way to secure distribution. If you can get your film accepted at one of the primary festivals (Sundance, Toronto, Cannes), you have a chance of attracting distribution. Individually, those festivals tend to attract more distributors than other festivals. Being at a competitive festival is good. You will find the psychology of the herd at work. If an audience likes a film or if one distributor becomes interested, all of a sudden a distributor feeding frenzy can start and prices go up.

Methods for Releasing Films

Few people invent new release strategies; they just refine the old tried and true ones over time. Some are in fashion, and some are out of fashion. When Peter Myers was senior vice-president of

Twentieth Century Fox Entertainment, he said that there were essentially two ways to distribute a film—fast and slow. That says it in a nutshell. All of the distribution books that you read (and you should learn as much as you can) will give names to procedures that are variations of fast and slow. I've added another speed, moderate, for our discussion.

Fast

The fastest way to release a film is to release it wide. Studios use this strategy for releasing many of their films when thousands of prints open simultaneously around the country. The wide release allows for a big opening weekend, which could have one of two outcomes. First, suppose a lot of people go to see the film, like it, and tell their friends. Assume the film opens on 2,000 to 3,000 screens. The average mall theater seats around 500 people, and the film shows three times a day. You have around a million people leaving the theater on a Saturday and telling their friends to see the film. The film develops excellent "legs," which means that it runs for a long time with good box office. The studios often use the results of the opening weekend as a measure of how much effort to put into promoting the film in the ensuing weeks.

The second possible result of a big weekend is that the same people leave the theater and tell their friends, "Don't go see that turkey." The film doesn't have legs or get extensive promotion. However, it does have that crowd of people who came opening weekend to see the star. The studio can use that in whatever advertising they do to lure more moviegoers into the theaters, before they hear any bad word-of-mouth.

Moderate Speed

In several standard patterns of release, a film opens in more than one theater at a time but in fewer than 500 overall. The standard definition for an independent used to be one that opened in 475 theaters or less. "Saturation," "platform," "rollout," and "sequencing" are variations on this theme. The film starts in a few selected theaters and moves on in some sort of pattern. A particular film may work best in one market because of the makeup of the population, because the film was shot there, or because the locals will go to see almost anything.

Films with difficult themes or at least an unknown audience may open in New York City or Los Angeles. The cosmopolitan nature and the size of the populations in those cities are an advantage. If a borderline film is destined to find any commercial acceptance, it will be in one of those towns. With good reviews, the film will continue to move through the country in one of several fashions. It might move to contiguous states, open in successive theaters based on a certain schedule, or cascade into the markets that are most likely to produce revenue. Whatever method is used, the film will continue to open in more and more theaters. Eventually, the number of theaters will decrease, but the film will remain in distribution as long as it attracts audiences. These methods have several advantages. They give unique films special handling, and they allow a popular-genre, small-budget film to move at the limit of its advertising budget. For example, if your film has a Native American theme, you can open in a moderately large city that also has a significant Native American population, such as Seattle. In this instance, the film plays to a special-interest audience in a town where the initial boxoffice dollars probably will give you a good start.

The goal of moderate-speed distribution is to realize sizable opening audiences (relative to the budget and theme of the film) and good reviews, then use the money and reviews to continue distribution. Clearly, no one expects a $3 million film to sell $17 or $20 million in tickets during the first weekend. The distributor may start with a few prints and fund the copying of more out of the revenues from the first few theaters. Advertising works the same way. Ads in a major city newspaper can run anywhere from $1,000 to $10,000. As a moderately budgeted film earns money, it finances the advertising in the cities to follow. For example, *Boys Don't Cry* opened on 2 screens, expanded to 22 screens, then hit a high of 365 screens after Hilary Swank's Academy Award nomination. The film, with a budget of $2 million, grossed $11 million in the U.S. Obviously the Best Actress nomination helped the final box office. Good word-of-mouth had already kept the film in the theater from October 8, 1999 until the nominations in February 2000.

Word-of-mouth is important in all release strategies. Had the initial audiences not liked *Boys Don't Cry*, it would have been pulled early and re-released after the nomination. Paul Dergarabedian, president of the box office tracking firm Exhibitor Relations Co. told Daily Variety, "Positive word-of-mouth is the manifestation of the positive feelings people have for a movie. You can buy an opening weekend, literally, with enough marketing hype. But the word-of-mouth is what is going to make or break a movie in the long-term."

Slow

The difference between slow and moderate-speed distribution is not necessarily the type of sequencing but the budget of the distributor. A very small distribution company may only be able to afford one print. Therefore, the film will start in one theater, and the distributor will "bicycle" it from theater to theater. Low-budget and no-budget films are promoted with this kind of marketing budget—exceedingly small. If a film attracts a larger audience than expected, they may sell the distribution rights to another independent with greater funds. I've seen a small company pick up a film at the Sundance festival and "flip" it to a larger company for a profit before the week is over.

"Four-walling" is another tactic that sometimes works with lower-budget films. In this case, the distributor rents a theater for a flat weekly fee and takes all the receipts. The gamble is that the total boxoffice dollars will be significantly greater than the guaranteed minimum to the exhibitor. Four-walling is used infrequently now, although occasionally a producer will self-distribute and revive this strategy.

Speaking of self-distribution, I try to dissuade most clients from doing it. Many don't have enough (or often any) previous business expertise to understand the dynamics. Sometimes filmmakers have no choice. No distributor wants the film. The filmmaker wants to gain better ancillary deals by exhibiting the film in a few theaters. As we have seen, occasionally the distributor runs out of money and can't afford to live up to an agreement for theatrical distribution. Investors will be very upset, if the film is never seen anywhere. However, even a modest theatrical distribution usually will mollify them.

There are several ways to approach this. Many filmmakers will put extra money into their budgets for marketing. If any of these funds haven't been spent, they can be used to get the film out. If the film is appropriate for a specialty theater, you may be able to screen the film for very little cost during one of the theater's down times. Localized publicity—flyer, the theater's newsletter—may get enough people into the theater to interest another distributor in picking it up. Or the original distributor may suddenly find available money he "hadn't noticed before."

Many producers have been successful at distributing their first films. If you speak with them afterward, however, they usually say they would not want to do it a second time. It should be done only out of necessity. Self-distribution carries a big risk for the producer, and the lack of skill can be downright dangerous.

Not to belabor the point, but distributors do have a body of experience, knowledge, and relationships that are hard to beat. If you think it is tricky to negotiate with one distributor, try negotiating with 30 in as many countries. The international market is a different deal in every country. You have to know how to structure the deals, what the censorship rules are, how you are going to get the money out of the country, and how to set up the mechanism to deliver the film. Even more to the point, experienced distributors know the bookers for the theaters—the people who actually accept the film for exhibition. At the very least, an individual should try to work in concert with a producer's representative to ease some of these complications.

Domestic distribution is not necessarily a picnic, either. The exhibitors have been in business a long time and are experienced negotiators. To check the receipts, you may have to stand at the box office and count the "house" as people buy tickets. Many filmmakers have taken a small film to a local specialty theater or two and shown that they can attract an audience. Then they are able to make a deal with a distribution company to take the film to more theaters. An example is *Claire of the Moon*. The producer showed the lesbian-themed film in a few theaters in San Francisco and then was able to make a deal with Strand Releasing for a wider release.

The 90/10 deal is a booking procedure that goes hand in hand with the release of small films. The distributor makes a deal with the theater to put up 90 percent of the advertising money and take 90 percent of the gross, after the exhibitor takes an agreed-upon minimum guarantee to earn the house "nut." This type of deal could be done at other percentages, but 90/10 is common. Distributors always try to negotiate the best deals they can get and afford.

FILMMAKER STRATEGIES

David versus Goliath

Many filmmakers let fate determine which way they will go in terms of distribution: studio or independent. This decision has no right or wrong answers, only options. The studio brings with it deep pockets, backup advice from experienced producers, strong marketing, and the ability to retain screens. Independent distributors bring an intimate knowledge of the low-budget market, the ability to disseminate films carefully over time, and a willingness to take a chance. Weigh your options carefully before making a decision.

There is a certain wisdom to the thought, "Just get the film made." Over the years, though, I have come to believe that raising money and making the film may actually be the easy part. Getting a good distribution deal for the film and financial deal for yourself and your investors is where the real work begins.

One filmmaker's meat is another's poison. Before going into any negotiations, be clear on your goals. The distribution decision is the major reason that you went through the exercise of listing your wants and desires in Chapter 2. You may seek advice and counsel from others, but in the end, you must make your own decisions. Table 6.1 helps you identify the pros and cons of studio and independent distribution.

The studio's backup system is a safety net for the new filmmaker. There are experienced producers on the lot, and executives are often dispatched to location to solve problems. This might be an advantage or a disadvantage. The independent filmmaker, on the other hand, usually completes the film before finding a distributor

TABLE 6.1
Pros and Cons: Studio versus Independent Distribution

	STUDIO	INDEPENDENT
Backup	A lot	A Little
Up-front Money	Generous	Little
Types of Films	Homogenized	Eclectic
Overrun Financing	Yes	No
Distribution Cutoff	Quick	Moderate
Bureaucracy	Heavy	Thin
Acquisitions	Sometimes	Preferred
Net Profits	Seldom	Sometimes
Producer's Capital	None	Some

and thus has far more freedom during the filmmaking process. Distributors generally do not have extra people to hang around the set and tell you how to direct or produce.

The nature of independent distribution supports smaller-budget films. In the studios, it is hard to make a film with a smaller budget. They've got unions, overhead, and extra costs galore. Independent distributors have to run a tighter ship. Certainly, when looking for financing, their goal is a small budget. The size of budgets for studio films usually leads to less imaginative and less chancy films being made. The independent system, meanwhile, embraces new and eclectic films. Studios maintain large bureaucracies, which make reaching a decision very difficult and time-consuming. The less cumbersome independent process enables quicker decisions because there are fewer chefs in the kitchen.

The studio's financial resources generally favor generous salaries for producers, directors, and cast. With independent films, above-the-line money is often cut to lower the budget to make it doable. Most studios assume a certain level of budget overrun with pictures and have the resources to support it. Conversely, private equity investors expect the budget you give them to be the final number. Underestimating can be dangerous because investors may not make up the shortfall. (More on this subject in Chapter 9.)

Studio distribution, as we have seen, is generally "get 'em out fast and wide." Historically, the studios have had neither the time nor the inclination to pamper a film through its release. It goes out everywhere with a lot of publicity. In addition, the studios have a short attention span. Films that fail to find their audiences quickly enough are pulled. Independent distributors, on the other hand, often have the knowledge and patience to give special care to eclectic or mixed-genre films. Many are geared to let a film find its audience slowly and methodically. Of course, there are some independent distributors whose forte is the mass-appeal genres. Most independents, though, have an expertise for releasing films with smaller budgets and lesser-known names.

The studios' desire to share in the small-film market used to last for only a brief time. Studios might go through cycles of acquiring smaller films, then forget about it. By buying indie companies, the studios have managed to stay in the niche market. These specialty divisions essentially act as they did previously, just with lots more buying power. For independent companies the niche markets are their business.

Earlier, we noted that your chances of a net profit on a studio film are low. There is a greater chance of having a real net profit at the end of the day with an independent film, although it is not guaranteed. The best policy in the movie business usually is to get what you can in the beginning—just in case.

The Control Factor

Filmmakers are well aware of the fact that studios retain the right to change anything they please—title, director's cut, and so on—and sometimes they assume that independent distributors will not want control over these things. Wrong! All distributors want to control the title and the cut. The only way to have total control over your film is to finance and distribute it yourself.

With the studios, the filmmaker's lack of control over projects is the stuff of which legends are made. Once your project goes into the system, it may be the last time you see it. If you are the writer, the finished picture may bear little resemblance to your original. Normally, there is far more control in independent filmmaking, but absolute control is a myth. An independent distributor will not allow you to have your way with everything. Novice filmmakers often are surprised at their lack of control. If only to protect themselves, distributors feel that they need these rights. Their biggest concern is to have a salable product, and, especially with neophyte producers and directors, they have no idea what they may be getting. A film that is too long, that drags in various places, or that includes scenes that were not approved in the original script will be a problem. Most independent distributors would rather deal with a finished film. That way, they know what they are getting before making an agreement, and they can request certain changes before obtaining the film. Of course, turning over a finished film is no guarantee for the filmmaker that no changes will be made.

Be Aware

When going into a distribution negotiation meeting, know what items are important to you. Talk to your attorney and get a feel for the deal-breakers—that is, the points on which you will not negotiate. No matter what someone says to you verbally, written agreements are what count. For example, if having a hand in the marketing is important to you, have it included in the contract. Be advised that many distributors will not want to concede this item. This does not mean that they will not listen to your input, but they want the final say.

Learn from the experiences of others. One novice filmmaker sent his distributor 40 minutes of finished film and 45 minutes of dailies. Although they had said that they wouldn't change a frame, they used the dailies to change the film to meet their standards. In addition, they took a frame from a scene that was not in the finished film to use for the poster. This allowed the distributor to promote the film as belonging to a different genre than it actually did. Will the average distributor do this? Probably not, but it is your responsibility to check out the people you will be dealing with to see how they have handled other filmmakers' projects.

In the last analysis, you must enter into the distribution agreement with care. Make sure your rights are spelled out. If you see the term "standard agreement," ask for a definition. Finally—and this cannot be said too strongly or too often—get a film attorney's advice before signing anything. I used to just say "entertainment attorney." But you need an attorney with experience in your industry. Whether it is film, television, music, book publishing, multimedia, or some other area, be sure that your attorney has experience specific to your needs.

Deliverables

While there isn't room in this book to go into all the aspects of distribution, I want to mention the delivery items. When you see the initial distribution contract and a small advance, remain calm. You have additional expenses. The filmmaker is responsible for delivering certain items to the distributor. Another reason for having that detail-oriented attorney. He will know whether or not those items are normally the expense of the filmmaker. They will include such things as 35 mm print, one-inch videotape, M&E tracks, music cue sheets, continuity script, MPAA rating certificate, E&O insurance policy copyright certificate, still photographs, and copies of all contracts and agreements. This is not a complete list but gives you an example. Often you have to provide multiple prints in different formats, as European countries use PAL. Before you sign, figure what all this is going to cost you.

WHAT DO YOU TELL INVESTORS?

The salient facts are here, but you must decide how much explanation to include. Always keep your description short and to the point. The Distribution section of your business plan should run four or five pages at most.

On the other hand, do say something useful. Your investors may know even less than you about distribution; as with other subjects, you have to dispel any wrong impressions they might have. Many investors think that their production financing gives them control of the distributor, too. In addition, some have been known to assume that the distributor will repay them all the production costs upfront before the film is released. These notions may prevent you from finding a distributor; in that case, no one will ever see your film.

Before you propose to take charge of all the marketing and promotion strategies yourself or decide to self-distribute your films, ask yourself a question: Who is going to make decisions? The idea may sound great—it will give you control—but there may well be pitfalls. If you do not know how to drive a car, what do you do after you turn on the ignition?

Getting a distribution deal is never a given. If you leave investors with the impression that distribution automatically comes with making the film, you may end up with a bigger problem than you ever imagined. I have seen many business plans that have a single statement—"We will get a distributor"—as the entire Distribution section. As you should realize by now, this approach is not the best. Do your research before writing your plan and explain the essentials. Then you will be in good shape to give investors confidence in your ability and your knowledge.

7

Risk Factors

A little uncertainty if good for everything.

HENRY KISSINGER
former Secretary of State

Every business plan requires a statement of risk in which you tell investors what a high-risk investment it is. Make it clear that nothing is guaranteed. No entrepreneur likes a risk statement, but it is a protection for you. In an LLC or limited partnership, your attorney will insert one whether you like it or not. You are well advised to do this in any proposal for funds. With a risk statement included in your business plan, investors cannot later claim that they did not know the investment was unpredictable. Even though it seems obvious to you, and probably to them, assume nothing and state the facts anyway. If things should go awry and people lose money, they tend to sue.

A risk statement can be a very short statement or a long explanation. In the business plan for one limited partnership, the risk statement ran 14 pages; this was a bit excessive. Where should you include the risk statement? I normally create a separate section. If you are at a loss for words, please borrow the one in this book. It can also be downloaded from www.moviemoney.com. Please use as is and only add the name of your film. Do not add sentences such as, "Our proposal has no risk, because it is sure to win an Academy Award." Or the ever popular "except our company" anywhere in the statement. You can put that anywhere else, except in the risk declaration.

RISK FACTORS STATEMENT

Investment in the film industry is highly speculative and inherently risky. There can be no assurance of the economic success of any motion picture since the revenues derived from the production and distribution of a motion picture depend primarily upon its acceptance by the public, which cannot be predicted. The commercial success of a motion picture also depends upon the quality and acceptance of other competing films released into the marketplace at or near the same time, general economic factors and other tangible and intangible factors, all of which can change and cannot be predicted with certainty.

The entertainment industry in general, and the motion picture industry in particular, are continuing to undergo significant changes, primarily due to technological developments. Although these developments have resulted in the availability of alternative and competing forms of leisure time entertainment, such technological developments have also resulted in the creation of additional revenue sources through licensing of rights to such new media, and potentially could lead to future reductions in the costs of producing and distributing motion pictures. In addition, the theatrical success of a motion picture remains a crucial factor in generating revenues in other media such as videocassettes and television. Due to the rapid growth of technology, shifting consumer tastes, and the popularity and availability of other forms of entertainment, it is impossible to predict the overall effect these factors will have on the potential revenue from and profitability of feature-length motion pictures.

The Company itself is in the organizational stage and is subject to all the risks incident to the creation and development of a new business, including the absence of a history of operations and minimal net worth. In order to prosper, the success of [*your film's name*] will depend partly upon the ability of management to produce a film of exceptional quality at a lower cost which can compete in appeal with higher-budgeted films of the same genre. In order to minimize this risk, management plans to participate as much as possible throughout the process and will aim to mitigate financial risks where possible. Fulfilling this goal depends on the timing of investor financing, the ability to obtain distribution contracts with satisfactory terms, and the continued participation of the current management.

8

Financing

*Raising money for a movie is like hitchhiking—It could be
the first ride, it could the thousandth. But you have to stay
out there with your thumb out and just wait. And you also
have to know when not to get into the car.*

..........Director JOHN SAYLES

Shuffle a pack of playing cards. Now spread them out face down,
and pick one card. If it is the ace of spades, you win; if it is not, you
lose. Your chances here of getting the right card are one out of 52.
These odds are better than the odds of finding independent money
for your film. Do not be discouraged, though. Many filmmakers
face these odds each year—and win.

Film is probably the worst investment anyone could ever
make. It is considered risky and capricious. If risks were measured
on a scale of one to 10, movies would rate a 15. One might as well
go to Las Vegas and throw the dice—in fact, those odds are probably better. Why would anyone invest in films, then? From a purely
financial standpoint, it is a gamble for which there is a big payoff.
In addition, there are many subjective reasons for investing in films
such as personal ideals, creative participation, and being part of the
glitter and glamour. The specific people and firms that are likely to
fund films change, but the modus operandi remains the same.
Some of the different sources of financing will be relevant for your
situation; others will not. Some are dynamic; some are static. As
studio executives and production companies go through cycles, so
do forms of financing.

By this point, you are well on your way to a finished proposal.
You have explained the basic information—your company and

product, the industry, the market, and the distribution process. You have your goals and objectives well in hand. Now here is the kicker. Popular agent lore (spread by agents) is that if a script is not interesting after the first 10 pages, it gets thrown in the "forget it" pile. Something similar can be said of investors and business plans. Investors typically read the Executive Summary first and the Financial section second. If they are still interested, they read all the delicious text between the two. This does not mean that all the in-between material is irrelevant, just that the primary emphasis is on the ins and outs of financing and how the numbers look.

When thinking about investors, most people picture a singularly rich person who swoops in and says, "Here's an extra $10 million I found in my drawer. Go make a film—no strings attached." Or, a country suddenly passes a law guaranteeing you 100 percent of your film costs just for showing up. This is the stuff of which movie plots are made. Not an impossible scenario, but an improbable one. You may get lucky early on, but it is more likely that there will be false starts, dashed hopes, and months or years of frustration.

As the saying goes, "If it were easy, everyone would be doing it." The truth is that finding financing is hard work. If you think otherwise, forget it. There are almost as many ways to finance a movie as there are people reading this book. We will look at specific methods, but note that the full financing of your movie may be a combination of several methods.

With a business plan for a new company, there is an additional struggle. Whether you are asking a money source to invest in one film or several, creating a feeling of confidence is not easy. Any anxiety on the part of the investor about funding one of your films is magnified when committing to finance an entire company. Besides making successful films, you have to be able to run that company. The investor will be looking with great care, therefore, at the management staff.

In your Financing section, you will discuss how your films will find financing, but you should do this without restating this entire chapter. Only certain financial strategies will be appropriate for your particular projects or for the type of investor you are going after. Too much irrelevant information will only confuse your reader.

This chapter examines some of the specific sources of money: single investors (rich people), presales, co-production and below-the-line deals, negative pickups, limited partnerships, and limited liability companies. In addition, it takes a brief look at bank loans. This chapter is meant to give you general knowledge of how film financing works; the intention is to make a complex subject easy to understand and to give you material for your business plan. It is not meant to be the complete and final word on the subject. For your own knowledge, do additional research on the specific financing techniques that you plan to use.

BEFORE YOU START

Before writing the Finance section of your business plan, there are several guidelines to think about and to follow. These concern the following:

- Seeking reality
- Finding the best fit
- Being careful what you promise
- Being careful what they promise
- Being able to explain it

Seeking Reality

The way that one person financed a film yesterday may not be relevant to you today. This appears to go against what was said earlier about learning from other filmmakers, but it does not. We said it was sometimes the same formula, not necessarily the same people. For example, suppose a filmmaker moves to Cincinnati, goes to play miniature golf, and meets a corporate executive. That very day, the corporation had decided to finance a film, so a deal is struck. That corporation may never fund another film. In fact, no one in Cincinnati may ever fund another film. Do not assume that you will find money in the same place. Learn from the other filmmaker's method, however; it may prove useful for you.

Finding the Best Fit

Filmmakers often believe that all money is equal; it isn't. Each source sets different requirements or conditions for the delivery of funds. You will be able to live with some of these, some not.

For example, there may be too many fingers in the pie. Three intermediaries later, you will be paying out huge sums. Or, prospective investors may have requirements that make getting the money not worthwhile. There may be content, length of time, or rate of return demands you cannot meet.

Worse, at the eleventh hour, Ms. Investor may inform you that her husband has to play the lead in the film. Don't be discouraged. The right source for you is out there somewhere; seek until you find.

Being Careful What You Promise

Making statements of absolute fact about financial conditions may be dangerous. An investor will hold you to whatever you promise. You might say, for example, "We will seek presales in order to recover at least some of the production financing up front." That is not a promise, only a statement of intent. On the other hand, saying to people, "We will obtain presale commitments," is a promise. Unless you have commitments already in hand, you may be making a promise that you cannot keep. And be careful of implied promises. If you want to tell them the reported Sundance purchase prices of *Tadpole* ($6 million) or *The Good Girl* ($4 million), be sure to say these are festival prices, which tend to be higher than distributors might pay at an individual screening in Los Angeles or New York. Also, resist the temptation to quote the $10 million price for *The Spitfire Grill*, which was at Sundance in 1996. I have seen investors refuse to approve a distribution deal because they assumed "normal" purchases were for twice the negative cost of the film.

Typical verbiage that I use is:

> *The other side of the spending equation is that often outsiders are not privy to the total deal. The price may cover a complete buyout, have a revenue cap, and cover any combination of territories. If the purchase is not a complete buyout, it usually covers exploitation rights for anywhere from 7 to 15 years, depending on the distributor and the territory. Although it is not possible to know the specifics of deals, it is logical to assume that this amount of money a total buyout with no other monies coming back to the investors in the future.*

Being Careful What They Promise

Always take the stance that you have to see it to believe it. People do not have to be con artists to lead you astray; many just like to hear themselves talk. Even investment bankers are seen bragging at cocktail parties about financing films they didn't. If a money source (finder or actual) is saying, "The check is in the mail," your mantra should be, "Do not spend any money until the cash is in the production account." This warning includes family friends and bank executives as well. If a source is promising a money-back guarantee, check the paperwork. If you are not knowledgeable about financial terms and clauses, find someone who is. Chances are, there is no guarantee at all. Look carefully in the fine print for how much cash this source is keeping. Do they have the resources to make such a promise, or are they making it on behalf of some other entity that has never heard of you and probably never will?

Being Able to Explain It

If you cannot explain a financing scheme, do not include it. To my constant amazement, I often receive business plans to critique that are based on a complicated financing structure, usually in a foreign country, that the producer does not understand or cannot find someone who has successfully used. Not just inexperienced film-makers but longtime professionals will base entire companies on such schemes. Frankly, not only are many of these too complex for me, but a majority either don't work or were fictional to begin with. Be especially wary if an intermediary wants a substantial amount of money in advance. If an investor on your side is required to make it work, you can bet your bottom dollar that your investor will ask for details about the financing with examples of companies that have used it successfully and a meeting with a principal (person that actually controls the other funding), so be prepared.

RICH PEOPLE: THEM THAT HAS THE GOLD

Investors are gamblers no matter what their reasons; and film is one of the biggest gambles you can find. Others have personal reasons. Private investors are equity players. They take a portion of the net worth of your company in exchange for their capital. Until you take in partners, you own the whole pie. As partners come in, you start to slice the pie into little pieces, and as the old saying goes, "Them that has the gold, makes the rules." The nature of an entrepreneur is to be filled with passion to accomplish a certain end. The hardest job for you may be your own emotional involvement when attempting to see things dispassionately from the investor's point of view.

Who Are They?

The first string of the investment team comprises friends and relatives. Raising development money and the negative cost of films under $1 million is very difficult. Professional investors do not see enough of a return on such small investments. Mom and Uncle Harry are more likely to be willing to give you a chance. Ed Burns raised the initial $20,000 for *The Brothers McMullen* with credit cards from family and friends. Kevin Smith funded the $26,575 budget for *Clerks* with credit card advances, the sale of his comic book collection, and a loan from his parents.

Entrepreneurs

Private money comes most often from people in businesses other than entertainment. Entrepreneurial types who have made a killing in almost any industry may feel the lure of film. It takes a high roller at heart to start a firm and prosper with it. You can try the annual Forbes 400 for a listing of billionaires; however, you may have to travel to Hong Kong or Taiwan to speak with them. You don't have to go that far for what you need.

Investors have all sorts of reasons for taking this risk. Some are after big bucks, some are personal fans, and some want to give back to the community. Despite their reasons, investors are seldom seeking to lose money. I have seen scores of creative people forget their dreams rather than face the reality that, whatever the content, these are business deals as well.

Art

Some investors want to be associated with "art." To this day, people will tell me that they want to make the Merchant-Ivory film *A Room with a View*. Unfortunately, they want to make it at 1986 prices and reap the box office of *My Big Fat Greek Wedding*. Merchant-Ivory probably also would like to be able to make a similar film for $1 million today.

In such a case, the investor's goals are unrealistic. You should make an attempt to create realistic expectations for him. If you are lucky, his desire to be associated with quality will outweigh the high return he wants for his investment. On the other hand, if he cannot afford more money and does not want to join with additional investors, move on. Put your energy into finding partners whose outlook and resources are a match for your project.

Special Interests

The line between business and altruism can be a thin one. Few people will become involved in a feature film without considering its commercial possibilities, but investors often have other reasons for funding. If you can find an investor whose sensibilities agree with the theme or purpose of your film, you may be able to create a workable collaboration.

Paul Sirmons' *The First of May* was funded by John Goodman of The Goodman Group. He felt the film was inspirational, and it was his way of giving back to the community. Goodman said,

> *When you're a child or an elderly person, without family, without a home, life can feel very sad and hopeless. But it doesn't have to be that way if you have a friend who cares. That's why I supported* The First of May. *It truly captures the spirit of joy that happens when two seemingly hopeless people, a lonely woman and a homeless little boy, rediscover, through each other, the hope life can hold.*

And don't forget nonprofit organizations. *The Spitfire Grill* was written to meet the needs of the Mississippi-based Sacred Heart League, a Roman Catholic charity, looking to invest money in a "spiritually uplifting" film. The film premiered at the 1996 Sundance Film Festival, where Castle Rock acquired the $6.1 million project for a surprising $10 million. The backers were happy. The film delivered their message of redemption and an immediate profit at the same time. Since then various secular faith-based groups have said that they were getting into the film business.

Many foundations and similar organizations have funded all or part of documentaries or feature films that fit with their particular mandate. The publicity given to this film inspired other religiously-connected groups to look at funding films. Having been involved with writing several business plans for filmmakers who were seeking money from religiously-oriented organizations, I caution you to be careful. Refer to the Goldwyn quote in Chapter 5. In order to get a substantial number of people to see your film, your first goal should be to entertain.

Foreign Investors

We hear a lot about European and Japanese investment in the American film community. In the early-to-mid-1990s, most of the foreign money went to studios or the formation of large production companies with experienced studio executives; $100 million was a favorite startup amount. From the late 1990s into 2002 German investment funds grew like crazy. Investors looking for prestige, profits, and extraordinary tax breaks began funding as much big budget output as they could. Some funds existed to fund studio films; otherwise financed independent companies, such as the U.K. firm Intermedia (*Iris, K-19: The Widowmaker, The Quiet American*). As some high-budget films failed and the economy started to collapse worldwide, many of these funds closed. However, new ones came to take their place. Any detail presented here would be out-of-date before you bought the book.

Generally, this money doesn't go to novice filmmakers. In tracking foreign money, you often run into "finders," people claiming to have a special relationship with foreign money. Some do; many do not. Remember to check these people out. A finder should be paid a percentage of the money you receive from the investor, and only after the cash is in your bank account. And, at the beginning of this journey, ask how many people are between the finder and the money. If that person is going through two other people to obtain the money, have them agree to split one fee. For example, if your finder's fee is 5 percent, then all three split that money; otherwise, you are paying 15 percent in finders' fees. Naturally, this is always your choice. But don't get backed into a corner to pay out three times what you intended simply because you didn't get the facts straight upfront. And whatever else you do, do not give them any money in advance.

Where Are They?

Your own backyard is the first place to look for financing. Few filmmakers are born in Los Angeles; they migrate there. Nor are the investors born in Los Angeles. They are born and live in Ohio, Michigan, Iowa, Texas, Maui, Florida, and so on. At least, those are areas where many of my clients have found investors. (Don't call me for a list; it's proprietary—nonpublic, company-owned—information.) You may find untapped markets of entrepreneurs with lots of money from very boring industries, to whom the lure of the film world may be irresistible. Your best chance is in an area where there is not a lot of competition from other filmmakers—if there still is such a place. The entire financing deal can be conducted without anyone living in Tinsel Town.

Giving a party is another strategy that I have seen some producers use to find interested investors. Since I am not an attorney, check the details with yours before proceeding. I have paraphrased some of the rules set out by Morrie Warshawski in his book *The Fundraising Houseparty* (available at warshawski.com). Although Morrie is focusing on raising money for nonprofit events, the same principles can be used for film fundraising:

- Potential investors receive an invitation to come to a private home.
- The invitation makes it clear that this is a meeting to launch a film.
- Participants arrive and are served some sort of refreshments.
- The host or hostess explains why they personally feel it is a worthwhile project.
- Participants sit through a brief presentation—appearances by actors in the films, script reading, etc.
- A peer (we might say shill) in the audience—someone articulate, respected, and enthusiastic—stands up and explains why she wants to be part of the project.
- Once you have established an individual's interest, you can contact them later about investing.

What You Get

Equity investors will want at least a 50 percent cut of the producer's share in the film; some may even want a higher percentage. No matter how many years you spent writing the scripts or how many hours you spent talking deals, it is their money. The 50/50 split is usually one of those "gold" rules. Before you start complaining, be glad your investors don't want 80 percent. Venture capital companies and professional film investors often require that much equity to put seed money into a company.

Before any profit splits occur, investors must be paid back for their investments. Many investors will allow a 90/10 split (in their favor) until that sum is repaid. They want to keep you alive in case there is reason for a second film. However, I have seen not just strangers but relatives as well insist on a 120 percent payback with interest before the filmmaker receives a penny. After the distributor and the investor are repaid, the producer's share begins—50 percent of the net profit, one would hope.

Filmmakers have a habit of promising "points" and film credits to people for their work in finding investors or getting the project made. Directors and stars who are too expensive for the film's budget often are given points as a deferment of part of their salary. These points all come out of the filmmaker's 50 percent. Investors are not responsible for any of these agreements unless they agreed to them ahead of time. Besides points, filmmakers like to give away credits. Be careful what you promise. Only a handful of investors want to remain anonymous; the majority want to see their name on the screen, and their credit of choice is Executive Producer. If you are going to look for investors, reserve this card for them.

Reasonable Risk

Entrepreneurs often want money from investors with no strings attached as a reward for their creative genius. They do not want to be responsible for how the money is spent or for whether investors realize a gain. No doubt, you are a genius. But do not expect to get financing without showing the investor what kind of risk she is taking.

Early in this business, I tried to get financing for an entrepreneur who had a new idea for using films for a specialized purpose in malls. One investor thought the project was "sexy" and that the idea could be taken national, but the business plan was so-so. The investor proposed to raise $5 million and look forward to a public offering (stock issue) for the new company. However, he wanted a revised business plan, and our client would have none of this. "After all," he said, "investors are supposed to take a risk. If these people are not willing to take one, who needs them? I'm not going to waste all this time. Big guys in New York are interested."

You can probably guess what happened. The client never heard from the "big guys," never got his company funded, and went back to his old job, never to be heard from again.

The moral here is not that people in New York are unreliable. Serious investors, whether they are in New York or Des Moines, will seldom make a final decision based on flash and dash. They want to see substance and detail. Even if someone likes your project, chances are you will hear, "Come back when you have the business plan."

The Big Payoff

The low-budget, big-return films are the hooks that lure many investors into the film business. Films like *The Blair Witch Project* and *My Big Fat Greek Wedding* will bring the high rollers into the financing arena. Very few other ventures, outside of Las Vegas, offer the potential of a 500–1,000 percent return on investment. As a filmmaker, you must be ready to show prospective investors that the chance of making a killing outweighs the risk of losing their money.

Remember, though, that you can never promise a risk-free investment. And you do not want to tell them, "Ten million dollars is typical of advances and/or buyouts for $1 million films."

When all is said and done, it is the projected bottom line that builds the investor's confidence. You need to find similar films and track their dollar returns. Whether you are looking at a single film or a company, you must project your revenues and expenses, box office grosses and rentals, and cash flows over the next 3 to 5 years. (You will learn how to do that in the next chapter.)

PRESALES

There are two main activities at the markets—AFM, Cannes, MIFED—seeking presales for as-yet-unmade films in order to finance production and selling finished films. We are concerned here with the former. The seller (you or your U.S. distributor) has a booth or room and entices the buyers from each territory and medium (theatrical, DVD, video, satellite, broadcast, and so on) to buy the ancillary rights (domestic or foreign) to your film in advance. (This is also called a "prebuy.") In return, you receive a commitment and guarantee from the prebuyers. The guarantee includes a promise from that company to pay a specific amount upon delivery of the completed film. If deemed credible by one of several specialized entertainment banks that accept such "paper," the contract can be banked. Then the bank will advance you a sum, minus their discount amount.

In exchange for the presale contract, the U.S. or foreign buyer obtains the right to keep the revenue (rentals) from that territory and might also seek equity participation. The agreement can be for a certain length of time, a revenue cap, or both. The time period can be anywhere from five to 15 years, with seven being customary. Many filmmakers are under the impression that "in perpetuity" (forever) enters into this negotiation. These terms are not unheard of, but they are more likely to surface if you are transferring the copyright, or ownership, of the film. There is nothing to keep people with money in their hands from demanding as much as they can get. The buyer tries to make the length of time as long as possible, and the seller tries to make it as short as possible. Be careful of the stance you take. Some foreign companies have told me that if the filmmaker balks at seven years, they will change the term to ten.

The "revenue cap" is a certain amount of money in sales, up to which the buyer gets to keep all the money. When negotiating these terms, buyers try to estimate the highest amount that the movie will make and then try to make that amount the cap. After the revenue cap is reached, the seller may start receiving a percent of the revenue or may renegotiate the deal.

Being the sole source of financing gives people much more power than if they are one of a group of funders. Yet any of these negotiations still depend on the "eye of the beholder." Any leverage depends on the desire of the buyer for the film.

Advances

Cable, home video, and television syndication companies have in the past been major sources of preproduction financing. Through advances, they fund all or part of a film's production in exchange for an equity participation and the rights to distribute the film in their particular medium.

Although advances do not occur as frequently as they did in the early 1990s, particularly in video, they are still a potential form of production financing. As noted earlier, though, most domestic distributors prefer not to see fractionalized rights. Always weigh this fact against the benefits of having an ancillary company as your main investor. The advance for a finished film is another matter. It may be a total buyout, have a revenue cap, or combine any number of characteristics common to presales.

Advantages and Disadvantages

The primary advantage of presales is that they offer you the chance to make your film. This source of money continues to be a workable one for new filmmakers. In addition, if you manage to reach your production goal over several territories, it lessens the impact that someone else can have on your film. Presumably, the fewer territories you presell or from which you receive advances, the more money you will be able to keep on the backend after distribution.

There are two disadvantages to this source of funding. First, you sacrifice future profits in order to make the film. Selling your film in advance puts you at a negotiating disadvantage. Companies that use presale strategies often give away much of the upside cash flow and profit potential from hit movies. Second, not all paper is bankable. You have to do a lot of research before accepting this kind of contract. Things change quickly, particularly in difficult economic times.

CO-PRODUCTION AND BELOW-THE-LINE DEALS

International co-production deals are the result of treaty agreements between countries. Qualifying films are permitted to benefit from various government incentives provided by the country in which production will take place. However, co-production agreements are not a charity event. A number of requirements may be imposed on the film by government treaty, including the following:

- The producer must be a resident of the host country.
- A certain percentage of above-the-line talent must come from the host country.
- A certain percentage of the technical crew must be residents of that country.

- Distribution must be done by a company located in the host country.
- A percentage of the revenues from the film must remain in that country.

Another type of co-production agreement can be made with a state or a production facility. Instead of providing hard cash (actual dollars with which to pay people), they provide studio time and equipment at large discounts or even free. Tied to these deals (and sometimes to the international arrangements), a company will provide below-the-line expenses ("soft currency") such as film stock, hotels, food, and the like. Various U.S. states, cities, and privately-owned studios have at some time offered co-production incentives. When studios were built in North and South Carolina, for example, their owners offered a break on studio and technical costs in order to attract business.

At various times, individual states have announced programs for supplying investment credits and/or prints and ads money for independent films in their states. The status of such deals is very fluid. By the time word spreads, the opportunity may be gone. Or maybe they weren't workable to begin with. Do careful research. Usually the state will have details of its program on its website. Currently, much attention is being paid to "runaway" films, such as those made in other countries due to good tax and rebate deals from the governments. With all of this, you have to decide if the bottom line really works for you.

Advantages and Disadvantages

The first advantage of co-production is that the total budget may be smaller because of the advantages of filming in a cheaper locale. Second, because of the readjusted budget, you will have to find a smaller amount of hard cash. The right deal will cover most if not all of your below-the-line costs. Many films would still be only a gleam in the producer's eye if part of the actual cash burden had not been removed by a co-production deal. In terms of disadvantages, you will still need to have hard cash for the above-the-line payroll—that is, the cast, director, writer, and production office staff. No film is made without these people, and they will not take I.O.U.s, although some take deferred salaries. Another disadvantage is that finding enough skilled personnel in a host country could be a problem. If you end up having to fly key technical people from the United States to another country or from California to another state, you may end up with a budget burden that offsets the advantages of the co-production deal.

NEGATIVE PICKUP

In the days when film companies had more cash, there were many negative pickups. The premise is that a studio or distributor promises to pay the cost of the film negative (production costs) upon delivery of the completed picture. This agreement is taken to the bank, which then provides cash for production at a discount to the total value of the agreement. A discount is a reduction in the stated value of the note.

The catch-22 here is that the bank has to believe that the studio or distributor will be able to pay off the loan upon delivery of the film (often a year from the date of the agreement). In the past, this was not as difficult to do as it is now. In the late 1980s, banks could count on the majors, a few of the mini-majors, and a very small number of distributors to make good on negative pickups. The entire situation has changed in the past several years. The financial problems of many of the large production companies are well-known. In addition, the troubles and, in some cases, complete collapse of many financial institutions have created an even more dismal picture. Nothing can be taken for granted. Although there are still companies that will give you negative pickups, this is not a financing strategy that I would count on. As with distribution deals, show the documents for your negative pickup to a bank to see if the deal is acceptable.

Advantages and Disadvantages

One advantage of negative pickups is that the film is made without giving away a share of the company to someone else. In addition, a negative pickup with a major studio or distributor removes the angst of searching for a distributor.

On the other hand, the standard negative pickup agreement contains two loopholes that favor the distributor. First, the agreement has a built-in escape clause that says, in effect, "You must deliver the film we were promised." Any change in the script, even if it seems minor to you, can cause cancellation of the contract.

Second, the contract also states that the finished film has to meet the distributor's standards of quality. Even if the movie is shot-for-shot the same as the script, the distributor can always say that the film's quality is not up to standards.

LIMITED PARTNERSHIPS

Until the mid-1980s, limited partnerships were all the rage. Subscribers could deduct losses calculated at many times the amount of their original investment; taxwise, therefore, the losses sometimes were more beneficial than making profits. In 1986, the Tax Reform Act removed most of these benefits, however, and now the investors have to pray for successful films.

A limited partnership has two kinds of partners. The General Partner, who is often called a "sponsor" or "syndicator," has unlimited liability with respect to the obligations of the partnership and is active in management. The General Partner chooses the investments and does not have to ask for the advice or agreement of the other partners. The Limited Partners, who provide all of the capital, share any profits or losses and are not actively involved in management. In addition, their liability is limited to the amount of their investment. Gains and losses flow through directly to the Limited Partners.

With a general withdrawal of investors from the market, limited partnerships in general and film partnerships in particular have had a more difficult time. The legions of medical groups to whom entrepreneurs formerly sold the documents became disaffected and moved on. The offerings are still a valid form of financing, but you may have to find your own investors rather than rely on brokers or other agents.

A public limited partnership must be registered with the SEC (Security Exchange Commission), and there must be a properly prepared prospectus that includes all the facts about the partnership. The prospectus must also include a business plan (be still, my heart!) and subscription documents. Limited partnerships can remain private if they are sold within a single state.

Do not write your own limited partnership agreement. Because of the cost of attorneys, film producers are fond of writing their own documents by cutting and pasting old ones. Do not do this. When it comes to fraud, working with unofficial documents is only one aspect. Any misrepresentation about the company's plans also constitutes fraud. The SEC and the Internal Revenue Service are not known for their senses of humor, and ignorance is not an acceptable defense.

Advantages and Disadvantages

On the plus side, the Limited Partners have no right to interfere with the creative process. Private placements provide a means to raise funds from multiple investors without having to negotiate different deals with each one. The subscription documents contain all the deal information. Los Angeles attorney Michael Norman Saleman prefers the limited partnership structure to limited liability companies. He says,

> The reasons that I prefer the limited partnership to the LLC have to do with the fact that the law does not adequately protect the LLC Member investors by limiting them to their investment as the total amount of their potential losses, as it does for the limited partner investors in a limited partnership. For example, California Law creates personal liability for LLC members if the LLC "veil" of protection is pierced, in the same manner as a corporation. That cannot happen to a limited partner. Also, there is nothing in the law that separates the control of the business from the managers and the members as it does between the general partner and the limited partners in a limited partnership. Finally, certain states, such as Texas, impose a franchise tax on LLCs and no franchise tax on limited partnerships. Therefore, by using a limited partnership in those states, a significant amount of potential tax liability is avoided for the investors.

There are disadvantages as well. Because of the complicated nature of all SEC regulations and the differences between public and private offerings, participating in one of these formats requires research and expert advice from an attorney. The law is complex, and ignoring any filing regulation (each state has its own requirements) may bring an order for you to cease and desist in your sale of the offering. Another disadvantage is that the producer or the purchase representative must have a previous relationship with the investor before approaching her or him with a specific offering.

Limited Liability Companies

In the past few years, a new financial structure, the limited liability company, has become popular. LLCs are a hybrid combination of the partnership and corporate structures. They are an attractive alternative to partnerships and corporations, because the LLC provides limited personal liability to the investors, who are referred to as "members." It also provides a single level of tax. In the standard limited partnership, General Partners (read "filmmakers" here) have personal liability for partnership debts, whereas Limited Partners in an LLC have no personal liability. The worst thing that happens is that they lose their investment. In addition, the Limited Partners cannot participate in management without jeopardizing their limited liability status.

In addition, an LLC member can participate in the entity's management without risking loss of limited liability. For federal tax purposes, the LLC generally is classified as a partnership. The same is true in "most" states—the operative word here being "most." I have clients who have formed an LLC in Michigan, for example, but not in Florida, where the LLC is taxed as a corporation. As there is no uniformity in the LLC statutes across states, creating an LLC with members in more than one state may be complicated. It is best to contact an attorney with experience in forming this new structure. Unfortunately, in this land of ours, the way conflicts become clear is through legal decisions in courts.

The LLC still does not have the body of law (i.e., court cases) behind it that the limited partnership does. When pass-through of revenue is of primary concern, strict conformance to IRS and state revenue accounting criteria should be considered before the LLC is chosen over the better-established partnership and "S Corporation."

Being Fair to Your Investors

When people invest in an LLC or a limited partnership, there is a payback schedule that is agreed to by both the filmmaker and investors. These agreements include the budget that you state in the financing documents. Attorney William Whitacre of Orlando, whose clients include Haxan Films and The Pamplin Film Company, says,

> In a limited liability company investors are passive; however, once the investment structure is determined and funds have been accepted, there can be no change in that structure, since doing so would dilute the interests of the initial investors. Accordingly, it is extremely important to budget accurately in the beginning before accepting investment funds into a limited liability company.

BANK LOANS

Bank loans are not associated with business plans per se. However, this discussion focuses on what you will tell potential investors, and bank financing may be relevant to your situation.

Banks are in the business of renting money for a fee. They have no interest in the brilliance of your potential films; they do not care that you are a nice person and have a sparkling reputation. By law, commercial banks (the ones that give you checking accounts) can only lend money based on measurable risk, and the only credit they can take is the collateral, or the assets being offered to secure the loan. The contracts that have already been discussed—negative pickups, distribution agreements, and presales—are such collateral (assets offered to offset the bank's risk). The bank does not have to worry about when you deliver the film or how the box office performs; it is the distributor who has that worry.

The cost of the loan is tied to the prime rate, which is the rate of interest that banks pay to borrow from the Federal Reserve. It is a floating number that may fluctuate significantly. Home lending rates, also based on the prime rate, are a good example. When the prime rate falls, everyone rushes to refinance their mortgages. In most commercial lending, loans to "low-risk" firms (e.g., major studios) can be one-half to 1 percent above the prime rate. On the other hand, a small production company, which represents a higher risk, would pay up to 3 percent above prime. Let's say that the bank is going to charge 2 percentage points above prime and that prime is 9 percent. The total would be 11 percent. On a $1-million loan, therefore, the bank removes $110,000 ($1 million multiplied by 0.11). To hedge their risk, the bank also retains another 1 or 2 percent in case the prime rate goes up. If the bank charges 1 percent, another $10,000 is added to their retained amount. Now you are down to $880,000 for the film. The bank is not through with you yet, however. It also charges you for its attorneys' fees, which can range from $15,000 for a simple contract to six figures if several companies are involved. Of course, you will still have to pay your own legal fees.

Once again we come back to the subject of attorneys. The one who represents you must know the ins and outs of all these contracts, so you should hire an experienced entertainment attorney. Costs go up drastically if your attorney is charging you an hourly rate to learn how the entertainment industry works. General corporate attorneys may mean well, but they can be an expensive choice.

Advantages and Disadvantages

The first advantage is that the producer is not personally liable for the loan; they can't take your house. A company is established for the production of the film, which is its only asset. In addition, many producers prefer to pay back a loan rather than give up equity. On the down side, the process to obtain a loan is expensive, and several parties and miles of paperwork are involved. Also, if the distributor defaults on the loan, the bank takes possession of the film.

COMPLETION GUARANTORS

Misunderstood by neophyte filmmakers is the role of the completion guarantor. This is not the person you go to for the rest of your production money; the guarantor's role is to provide an assurance that the film will be completed and delivered to the distributor. The contract with the producer or distributor allows the guarantor to take over the film to complete it if need be.

For the bond itself, the guarantor charges a fee based on the film's budget. The charges have been flexible over the last few years, depending on the state of the completion business. The bond is not issued until after funding is in place, however, and this is often a difficult fact to explain to investors. To make matters worse, small films have trouble getting bonded anyway. The risk is too great for most guarantors to bond low-budget films. In the past few years, several of the biggest bond companies lost their financing from insurance companies when high-budget films failed. The active companies had their hands full with major productions, leaving little time or inclination to consider your $1 million film. New companies have come into the market, making the completion bond more accessible for some smaller films. However, their staying power depends on the insurance companies that back them.

In most business plans, I no longer mention a bond, as I know they have no chance of getting one. However, depending on the budget of a film, I will say that the filmmaker "intends to seek a bond." Never promise one, if you don't already have it.

A completion bond is always desirable to protect both you and your investors financially. Accidents and bad weather can happen. They have the right to decide what exposure they want to have. As always, honesty is the best policy with your investors and yourself.

WHAT DO YOU TELL INVESTORS?

A section on financing techniques is required as part of your business plan package. Give investors only relevant information, not everything in this chapter. Based on the assumption that your readers are not film sophisticates, you should explain what constitutes a presale agreement, a negative pickup, or whatever form of financing you will pursue. Be prepared to answer investors' questions. They may ask you about the forms of financing that you have not included. You should be conversant enough with the pros and cons of various strategies to explain your choices intelligently.

As mentioned earlier, it is unproductive to include financing methods that you do not plan to use. If you plan to use a limited partnership, for example, the business plan will be part of the offering; otherwise, there is no reason to discuss this form of financing. To do so would be to create a red herring for investors, confusing them with a nonexistent choice. Along the same lines, you should be careful about considering options that may no longer exist. What Canada or Australia is doing in 2003 may not be relevant in 2004 or later. Financing patterns, like everything else in our culture, can be in or out of vogue from year to year. It is important to keep current with the business climate through the trades and other sources while writing your plan.

Paul Sirmons says,

> *The most important thing an independent filmmaker must realize is why an investor puts money into an independent movie. He is investing in you, in his belief in that you can actually deliver everything you tell them as a finished, professional movie. They must believe that you really can pull together the story, the script, the actors, the crew, the shoot, the post-production, and the distribution deal. If you don't feel that you can convince people to believe in you, then partner with a producer who has those skills ... but passion is also important. It will give the investor that extra confidence to invest in your movie. And the patience to wait for the returns. And wait. And wait.*

The Financial Plan

9

Get your facts first; then you can distort them as you please.
MARK TWAIN

FORECASTING WITHOUT FEAR

Predicting the future has been popular since the days of Nostradamus. No one can afford to run a business without looking ahead. Only when you have a clear picture of your company's potential growth can you proceed with a feeling of confidence. In the past 500 years, little has changed except the technology. For filmmakers, predicting the revenue of films yet to be made is a necessity. This chapter reviews how to find data, what to do with it after you find it, and how to create your own financial forecasts.

Students often object to looking up boxoffice grosses for a class assignment. Their idea of a business plan is a description of their films and, possibly, general market and distribution information. Although important, these items pale in importance to projected income. Remember the investors? They are going to read the Executive Summary first and then go quickly to the revenues and expenses. Money is the glue that holds these building blocks together. Before investors hand over hard cash, they want to believe that your project will be profitable.

Forecasting is an art, albeit not a precise one. Sophisticated business writers like to say that the one sure thing about a prediction is that it will be wrong; they are probably right. The value of a forecast is as a guide for making decisions; the better informed the forecaster, the closer to actual events the forecast will be.

By researching history, looking for relationships among the data you find, and making assumptions about the future based on those relationships, you have a basis for predicting your future grosses.

When writing your proposal, you have to decide which group of numbers tells your story best. The most recent data may be a year or two behind because of the flow of revenues. You therefore have the opportunity to forecast to the current period, putting whatever spin on these statistics you feel is justified. Your description of independent distribution should involve more than just how many films there were and how much money they took in as a group. Your goal is to show that the independent film market is robust and that profits have nowhere to go but up.

Anyone Can Do It

There is no mystery to forecasting revenues and expenses. You do not have to be an accountant or hold an M.B.A. You do not need a previous knowledge of trend analysis, regression and correlation points, or internal rate of return. This jargon is used by financial whiz kids to speak to one another; life can go on without it. The information that you uncover can be used to create the numbers that make a company look feasible. You will take the elements that seem to influence the outcome of a film—genre, stars, director, distribution, ancillary returns—and analyze how much you think each will influence the resulting revenue. The only math skills you will need are adding, subtracting, multiplying, and dividing. Mix these skills with a little gut feeling, and you have a forecast. If you can balance your checkbook, you can create a forecast.

FINDING THE DATA

In predicting the future revenues for your films (or other projects), you need to know what has happened in the recent past (five years). Where do you look? You might try trade papers, industry magazines, regular newspapers and magazines, festivals and film markets, seminars, and other industry meetings. These sources were discussed in Chapter 5, "The Markets and Marketing."

Let's look at some specific data that you can uncover in your research. Every Tuesday, the trade papers (*The Hollywood Reporter* and *Daily Variety*) publish the 60 top-grossing films for the previous week through Sunday. The boxoffice grosses in these tables equal the total domestic gross sales for the film. Since they include Canada, the grosses are really North American, but for convenience we will refer to them as U.S. grosses. The majority of the films on the list used to be studio productions. However, for the last few years, 30 or more of those films in any given week are independent. With the increasing propensity of studios to become co-financing partners with less than 50 percent of the film, more of the films are independent than we can easily identify.

Since the last edition of this book, both *Variety* and *The Hollywood Reporter* have put the North American grosses online. With a subscription, you can track the domestic box office for films in *Variety* from March 1994. For foreign box office, complete data is available for sixteen countries from March 27, 1997 for major territories. *The Hollywood Reporter* has the current box office online as well as the current totals for ten countries.

Now you have a beginning. Let us say that you want to know the boxoffice totals, number of screens, and other figures for *Frida*. The most recent data is for the weekend of April 20th. The U.S. box-office gross (remember, this includes the exhibitor) is $25,776,062. The film is on 62 screens down 25 from the previous week. If you want to follow the revenue from the beginning, search for the film in the box at the top of the page. You will get the data from the weekend of October 25–31, when the film opened for $323,073.

The boxoffice grosses are collected and estimated by a company called Entertainment Data, Inc. (EDI). Because the weekly lists contain no more than 60 films, a film might continue in release but not have a high enough box office to appear on the charts for its entire theatrical run. Experience shows that the trade lists give a majority of the grosses. Occasionally, a film will reappear on the list as it begins to rise in total box office again. Lists published annually give a total recap of many of the film grosses, but you may not have the time to wait that long. If you do not subscribe to the trade papers online or in print and your local college library does not have them, check the major booksellers. Many of them carry *Weekly Variety* and sometimes the daily trades.

I also encourage clients and students to call the producers of the film in which they are interested. Independent filmmakers are very generous with one other. Having someone interested enough in your film to call is very flattering. Alternatively, you might call the distributor, if it is a smallish company. Distributors love to report high grosses. Budgets are another story. Depending on whether the filmmaker is looking for a distributor or wants to brag about how well the grosses have done on a low budget, you may or may not know the real budget. Unfortunately, the revenue is only part of the story. A $24.6 million gross with a budget of $6.5 million is a lot more impressive than it would be with a budget of $10 million. You have to go with the best information you can get. Try not to make them up. There are enough resources out there to find a reference to the budget. If you are really into keeping your own database, the U.K. trade paper *Screen International* is another good resource.

Again, interviews with filmmakers in the public press are a good source. Check the week or two before release. For recent film releases, check television and radio shows for the appearance of a filmmaker. Young filmmakers appear often on the morning and evening talk shows. Watch CNN, E! Entertainment Channel, *Oprah, Charlie Rose,* and all the news programs, especially on the all-news channels. In recent years, the Independent Film Channel and the Sundance Channel have gone on air in selected markets; naturally, they are dedicated to information about independent films.

The film festivals are another place to gather extensive financial information. Many producers and directors of independent films attend, and they will usually answer questions about not only the cost of their films, but also the source of their financing. People often feel more comfortable about revealing proprietary data face-to-face. Also watch the Oscar telecast and the Cannes Film Festival Awards (broadcast on Bravo). You never know what you might learn.

What about older movies? To check what you can find, I had financial analyst Faryl Saliman Reingold research grosses and budgets for a selected list of films that were released before 1990. *Off Hollywood* by David Rosen and *Making Movies* by John Russo contained some of the data we needed. Then she went to the library and checked the periodical indices under the names of the directors and the films to locate relevant interviews and articles. In addition, she checked the trade papers for the year of release of each film. We were able to obtain enough articles and figures from the *New York Times, Newsweek,* and *Variety* to complete the table. Now some of the information can be found on the Internet.

Now that you have the box office and budget figures, you can estimate the rentals (review the tables in Chapter 4, "The Industry"). It has been assumed that 50 percent is the studio's average share of the box office and that 50 percent (up from 49 percent since the last edition of this book and 45 percent from the early to mid-1990s) is the amount returned to the independent distributor. In working with these numbers, it is necessary to use the average return. If you are projecting your own film with a specific distribution or booking method, then you can figure that into your equation.

Foreign and Other Data

Foreign rentals of independent films are harder to obtain. The handiest published sources for international dollars are the charts in *Weekly Variety* and *The Hollywood Reporter*. However, because these papers cover only the top 10 films in each country, more high-budget studio films than low-budget independent films can be tracked this way.

The vast majority of foreign theatrical revenues arrive within 15 to 24 months of the U.S. release. For your purposes, using the total return is acceptable. You can also use Table 9.1 to get an estimate on each country. Keep it to yourself, however, and only give your investors total foreign numbers. If anyone expects you to estimate each country separately, resist the urge. You may be painting yourself into a corner; remember what we said about implied promises?

Revenues from cable, free television, video, and other ancillary sources are published in the individual industry trade journals and newsletters. To find the results for specific films, you may end up having to spend money on an Internet subscription service, such as baseline or a consultant such as Business Strategies. Magazines published specifically for the video and cable industries are also a source of data. Check local libraries, especially at the film schools, to see what information they carry. Occasionally, U.S. and worldwide numbers are reported in articles that sum up the past year. You may also be able to find models, such as the one in Table 4.2. Models are not meant to represent any particular film but give you a measure of the average. They are published in books and occasionally trade papers.

Average Foreign Revenues

Several sources provide the latest information on typical revenues from individual foreign territories. *The Hollywood Reporter* prints

TABLE 9.1
Potential Sales by Territory for Budgets
up to $1.5 Million ($ Thousands)

COUNTRY	HIGH	LOW	AVERAGE
<u>Asia</u>			
Japan	70	20	45
Indonesia	20	10	15
Korea	75	15	45
Hong Kong	30	10	20
India	20	10	15
Taiwan	45	10	28
Philippines	30	10	20
Other	<u>30</u>	<u>15</u>	23
Total Asia	<u>320</u>	<u>100</u>	210 *
AustraliaNew Zealand	50	25	38
<u>Europe</u>			
Great Britain	70	35	53
Germany	65	30	48
France	80	45	63
Italy	65	30	48
Scandinavia	55	25	40
Spain	50	20	35
Holland	15	5	10
Other	<u>100</u>	<u>30</u>	65
Total Europe	<u>500</u>	<u>220</u>	360 *
<u>South America</u>			
Brazil	30	10	20
Mexico	50	20	35
Other	<u>55</u>	<u>25</u>	40
	<u>135</u>	<u>55</u>	95 *
Middle East	30	10	20

Note: Sales dollars courtesy of various distributors
* Do not total the averages.

"The Going Rate" in their AFM and Cannes product editions. The films are divided into budget categories, such as $750,000 to $1 million, $1 to $3 million, $3 to $6 million, and $6 to $12 million. The classifications depend on who has provided the list. They provide high and low prices for theatrical films.

The American Film Marketing Association releases a table of global sales every year that is reprinted in several industry papers and magazines. In addition, some of the foreign trade magazines gather data. Usually, these numbers are released around the time of the American Film Market and can be obtained there quite easily. You might also research the trade papers for late February and early March, when the market is held. Table 9.1 is a compilation of average territory sales gathered from individual distributors. These numbers are not boxoffice totals, but represent the average advances from distributors in that territory. As this may be the only money you ever get from them, you can use it to get a general idea of your prospects. The range of likely prices is based on the distributors' experience in selling low-budget films. When forecasting, you always want to be conservative, so you would use the average return of dollars. For example, looking at Japan, you see the high is $70,000 and the low is $20,000. This does not mean that all distributors will pay you $70,000; generally, the most they will pay is 10 percent of the budget. Use the average figure, which is $45,000.

What Has Happened?

There is no question about it: You must analyze this data before putting it into your proposal. I have said it before, but filmmakers have convinced me that I cannot say it too often. This analysis is your job, not the investor's. Do not expect the investor to accidentally happen upon useful information while browsing through the 15 or 20 pages you have photocopied from newspapers and magazines. It is your duty to find useful information and present it in an easily understandable way.

The data that you gather about previously released films will serve two purposes: (1) show the profits (if any) of films recently released, and (2) supply a basis for estimating the revenues for your films. The first part of your numerical story consists of showing what has happened with films that have already been produced and released. You use these examples to build a case for the ultimate success of your film. Select recent films that have a relation to your planned production in terms of genre, budget, or other common factors. Try not to go back more than five years, as changes in box office make older films less comparable. If you are dealing with a new or recent genre, of course, you may not have this option. For example, because *The Blair Witch Project* was a pseudo-documentary and there were no recently successful mock-umentaries, we had one table of feature-length documentaries and another table of low-budget films. Since *Scream* was a $10 million film and *This Is Spinal Tap*, the most successful mockumentary up to that point, was too old (1984) for the numbers to be comparative, both of those films were discussed in the Market Section.

Genre is a common way to group films; however, use what-ever characteristic you feel links these films together. But whatever your rationale for grouping films, use budget clusters that make sense. If your film has a $1.5 million budget, films in the $30,000 to $5 million range are okay. If you used $1 to $2 million, there would be few films. If you go over $5 million, you will have films that have elements you cannot match, such as better production values, cost of prints and ads, and quality of cast. With the advent of digi-tal film, this concept is becoming increasingly more difficult for filmmakers to comprehend. At this point, of course, there aren't enough films to compare. When your $30,000 is upped to 35 mm, what will it really look like? Try not to fantasize for a moment. Is it really going to look like $5 million on the screen? Will it have the same cast that a $5 million film will have? When comparing your film to other movies remember that the audience doesn't care how you made the film, but what it looks like and who is in it.

The films you include in your business plan depend on what is available. It is your choice whether to include films that have lost money. There is no database that includes all the films ever made, so you can't have a "fair" sampling no matter what you do. However, if you only use five films but they are all films with extraordinary results—*Four Weddings and a Funeral, Life Is Beautiful, Il Postino, Fargo,* and *The Blair Witch Project*—any projec-tion you make will be unrealistic and recognized as such by most investors.

Whatever tact you take, heed this warning: DO NOT INVENT NUMBERS. If lying does not bother you, getting caught in a lie will. Then the game will be over. If boxoffice grosses are all you can find, then that is what you must use.

Tables 10.1 through 10.6 included with the sample Business Plan (see Chapter 10) are examples of methods for presenting this information. Tables 10.1 through 10.4 show comparative films. Table 10.5 shows the revenues and expenses for each film, and Table 10.6 shows the cash flow over time. The films listed in the table are fictional, but based on the actual results of real films. These sample tables include the following items:

1. *Domestic theatrical rentals*: Domestic rentals are the portion of the U.S. theatrical box office that reverts back to the distributor (or producer). (The tables in the trades commonly include Canadian boxoffice figures in this total.) If only boxoffice figures are available, you can assume 49 percent of the total for this number. For individual films, it could be a little lower or higher.

   When working with numbers, you should avoid factoring in exceptional movies that would make all your averages too high. If you want to include *The Blair Witch Project*, list it and indicate in a footnote that it is in your chart for reference only. On the other hand, if you have a $10 million film, forget it. Just as on any given day any team can win, it is theoretically possible for any film to be a breakout hit. For purposes of estimating and projecting, however, you should use more typical results. Mark Twain said, "There are three kinds of lies: lies, damned lies, and statistics." Reflect on this.

2. *Domestic ancillary revenue*: The ancillary revenue includes all nontheatrical sources, such as cable, video, DVD, free television, syndicated television, and pay-per-view.

   Video was already diminishing as a source of advance money in the last half of the 1990s. The distributors are now trying various formulations of revenue-sharing as opposed to paying per unit. However, it is too early to know the effect on independent film. Pay-per-view (movies on demand) is growing, although not as quickly as analysts have expected. The windows for cable have changed and the premium channels are getting movies sooner than they used to.

   Unless you have a deal in the works, do not plan on advances from cable. HBO and Showtime normally only advance money on films being made for their own use. Be aware that although a few of the indie films financed by cable networks have had a U.S. theatrical release, most do not. In the past, PBS has also financed films that have had a theatrical release prior to being shown on television. There is no indication, however, that this strategy is a general policy. In addition, as new executives take charge, policies often change in both network television and cable.

3. *Foreign theatrical revenue*: The distributor is responsible for collecting money from the foreign box office, which includes all countries except the U.S. and Canada. Some films that do only moderately well in the United States do much better overseas, although generally the U.S. theatrical results drive the foreign box office. If a picture does not perform well in U.S. theaters, it normally makes all other theatrical and ancillary venues worth less money.

   The type of film and the stars often have a lot to do with these results. Certain U.S. television stars continually appear in movies-of-the-week, for instance, because they have large followings in foreign markets. This fact does not mean that distributors will accept them in your feature films. There are other films that do well in domestic and foreign video but have weak theatrical box offices.

4. *Foreign ancillary revenue*: Foreign ancillary presents great opportunity. Television companies often buy exclusive product. In addition, markets have opened up in Eastern Europe and Asia. Distributors report that Southeast Asia and India are becoming much stronger as revenue sources. The potential revenues for English-language films, even small ones, in other countries remain much stronger than for foreign-language films in the United States.

5. *Total revenue*: Rentals plus domestic ancillary plus foreign equal total revenue. The foreign dollars are assumed to have the exhibitor portion removed and, therefore, can be added to the domestic dollars to find total revenue. Always be sure that you are comparing apples to apples.

6. *Negative cost, prints and ads, and total costs*: We have already discussed finding the production, or negative, costs of the film. These are not the total costs, however. Prints and ads are an important expense. It is necessary to include these costs to get a total profit picture. As films stay in distribution, the P&A costs grow. Therefore, if you are forecasting the initial release cost, indicate it. The most credible source for this type of information is baseline.

7. *Gross profit (loss)*: Gross profit (loss) equals the revenue minus the direct expenses before the company operating expenses. In this case, direct expenses are the negative and prints and ads costs. They relate directly to your film, as

compared to the company overhead costs, which exist whether a film is in production or not. Notice the parentheses around the word loss. When preparing financial statements, use parentheses rather than minus signs to indicate negative numbers. Both words can be written on the profit line. However, if there isn't a projected profit, you may want to rethink the whole idea.

WHAT TO DO WITH THOSE PESKY NUMBERS

Now we come to your films. Here are two guidelines for projecting your revenues. First, be conservative. The rule of thumb is to forecast your income on the low end and your expenses on the high end. Probably all filmmakers who have ever done a budget have padded it to be sure that they did not run out of money. You want to take the opposite path for revenues. If you are making a $3-million black-themed film from the viewpoint of the "bad kids," you may be overly optimistic to assume that the film will gross close to $30 million, as *Menace II Society* did. For one thing, that film was at the Director's Fortnight at Cannes. It is nice to aspire to be accepted at such a prestigious festival, but you can't plan on it. Bring your average revenues down at least $10 million to be on the safe side.

Second, be honest. As long as the data of your historical films are as accurate as possible and the films you choose are comparable to those you plan to make, you should be all right. The comment made to me most often by distributors and investors is, "Tell them not to include *My Big Fat Greek Wedding* and *The Blair Witch Project* as average films." Feel free to discuss them in your analysis as an example of an exceptional result to hold out the brass ring as a hook for the investor. As long as you use those terms, you will be okay. You think I am being repetitive? You're right. It is an important point.

Assumptions

Before seizing your calculator, you should write down your assumptions. Unless you have concrete reasons for the forecasted revenues in your tables, people may assume that you invented them. There has to be a thought process leading to these numbers. If you have just written 15 or 20 pages for the preceding sections, you have already gone through the thought process. In most cases, the crucial elements have already been mentioned, and the list is a recap for your benefit and for the investor's. Do not expect readers to remember the specifics from the body of the business plan; this is not a game of hide and seek with the investor.

Explain your assumptions at the end of your Financial Section, directly before the tables, to be sure that the reader knows how you came to your conclusions. If you do not do this, it may look like you have no rationale. Review the assumptions in the sample business plan before continuing.

Revenue and Expenses (Income Statement)

The Estimated Income Statement (Table 10.5 in Chapter 10), also known as the "Statement of Revenues and Expenses," is the profit statement for the company as a whole. The sample shows a straight-forward production company in which all the income is from films. If you are planning to produce other products, such as video, you will need several revenue lines to show each product separately. You should also provide separate assumptions and cash flows for those products because they function differently from film. Then make a combined statement that includes all the products.

Looking at the numbers, you can take the average of all the films or the median (the point above and below which half the films fall), or you can give more weight to the more recent films. It depends on whether you feel that the genre is gaining more audience approval or has been drawing the same amount of boxoffice dollars for the past few years. You have to look at the available data and use good judgment.

Note that these tables show worldwide results. As you will not have these for the two most recent years, you want to include a table that shows the box office and budgets only for those years.

The net profit (loss) line is the sum of the company's revenues and expenses. Commonly, the phrase "before taxes" is added to indicate that this is a preliminary income forecast. Do not let these phrases throw you. An accountant can easily prepare these statements for you.

Cash Flow Statement

A cash flow statement shows the timing of incoming revenue and outgoing cash. The dollars will not come in all in one week or one month. Table 10.6 shows a sample cash flow statement. Notice that in the columns for the table, I have used generic terms "Year 1," "Year 2," "Year 3," and so on. If you are looking for the production money, your year starts when that money is in the bank. To specify the first year—for example, "2004"—could create a problem. What if you are still wandering around two years later looking for money? Finding money is hard; no need to announce it to your current prospect.

In addition, each year is further divided into quarters. This seems to make the most sense for showing cash flow. However, you can use whole years. I would shy away from individual months. The format is hard to read and includes more detail than is necessary. Unless you have the distributor's monthly accounts for various films in front of you, there is no way to track such data accurately.

In the sample cash flow statement, all of the production money is outgoing in Year 1. I have assumed one year from the beginning of production to the end of post-production. If you are an experienced filmmaker, you may be able to shorten this time frame. Release of the film is scheduled for six months after the end of post-production. No one really knows the actual timing in advance, even if you already have a distribution agreement in place. But we are using estimates, not promising a specific interval. Note there is the following comment at the bottom of the table: "For reference only. How and when monies are actually distributed depends on contract with distributor."

The first rentals are shown during the quarter in which distribution begins. For this edition, we did a study on independent films in 2002. Most of them were in domestic theaters for six months or less, with a majority of the revenue returned in the first quarter. Track domestic grosses week to week to find trends in the number of theaters and the amount of grosses. Going through that exercise will reveal a pattern that you can use. Average release "windows" give you an idea of the money flow from other sources. Again, not all films are released the same way. Some countries actually legislate the time period; in other cases, the distributor negotiates it. Trying to figure this out country by country would be excessive. The timing has been very fluid lately, so it is a good idea to research the topic to keep current. The films go into foreign release in the third quarter of Year 2, approximately seven months after the domestic release date. All the foreign revenues have been grouped into one category. The films go into domestic ancillary markets at the same time. The current release pattern is still video and pay-per-view, followed by other cable channels. Keep your eye on the news, however; changes are in the wind.

The total line is the sum of the incoming cash minus the outgoing cash. Because the production costs for the second film begin in the second year, production and prints and ads expenses appear as a deduction from the incoming cash flow. In a multi-picture company, the cash flow statement allows you to see whether you will have enough money coming in to keep production going. Do not panic over minus totals. The amount of eventual profit is the deciding factor.

The cumulative total is simply the sum of the totals from quarter to quarter, showing the position in profit and loss. These numbers represent the profits and losses from the films only. To keep the table simple for our purposes, the company overhead numbers have not been included; however, you need to include them for the overall company picture. In real life, ongoing costs that cannot be assigned to a specific picture must be included to show the company's total cash position at any point in time.

RUNNING THE COMPANY

An ongoing company has its past history to report, along with a statement of its present position. Your accountant will do the serious reports for you, such as Sources and Uses of Funds, Balance Sheet, and so on. These go into your Financial Planning section along with the other tables. As new companies have less to report, don't worry. Just report what there is. There may or may not be a bank account worth mentioning. Present information that must be included in the business plan, even for a very small company.

Administrative (Overhead) Expenses

If you are setting up a company, you will have ongoing expenses, no matter what films you are making. Your company's overhead will be

far less than that of the studios, of course. These gene
tive costs include salaries that are not attributable t
budget as well as all of the company's tools of t
equipment, telephone charges, entertainment costs, ana ১৬ ৬-
company may have fewer people or no salaried employees at all.
Before Year 1, there are generally start-up expenses. You may rent an
office, option a script, buy a computer, or scout locations in the
Dardanelles. Any expenses that are necessary to get your company
going are shown in this table. Even if you wait for investment funds
before doing any start-up, list these costs separately. Some of them—
like the computer—are one-time costs.

Like everything else, administrative costs are projected over
the time period of the business plan. Look ahead to the number of
films that you plan to make three or four years down the road. You
may need additional office staff, more office space, or increased
development money. Everyone knows that these numbers are
guesstimates; however, as a general rule, you should include all the
expenses you can think of. On the other hand, do not give yourself
a salary of $1 million. I see this item in a lot of companies that never
get funded. Because you are partners with the investor, your salary
should be moderate.

WHAT IF I HAVE ONLY ONE FILM?

Sometimes people are confused about the sample business plan in
Chapter 10, because they only have one film. I have used three for
those who are starting a larger company. As a filmmaker (producer,
director), you are the manager of a small company. The difference
is that you will be able to charge all of your expenses to the film.
Don't over- burden this poor film with your car and house payments. Include only those things that belong in a film budget.

The layout is the same for one film as for multiple films, but
fortunately you have less number crunching. Your first table will
be comparative films for the last three years (or four if you need
them) for which you have worldwide numbers. Your second table
will be the two years for which you only have U.S. box office and
budgets. Then you have an income statement (without the overhead) and a cash flow statement, which will be similar to any of the
individual films in the sample business plan.

THE NEXT STEP

Review Chapter 1, "Executive Summary," then study the sample business plan in Chapter 10. Then work through the sample on the CD. Feel free to use this format as a guide in writing your own plan.

Have fun, and good luck!

Sample Business Plan for a Fictional Company

CRAZED CONSULTANT FILMS INTERNATIONAL

THE BUSINESS PLAN

This document and the information contained herein is provided solely for the purpose of acquainting the reader with Crazed Consultant Films International. It is proprietary to Business Strategies. This business plan does not constitute an offer to sell, or a solicitation of an offer to purchase, securities. It has been submitted on a confidential basis solely for the benefit of selected, highly qualified investors and is not for use by any other persons. By accepting delivery of this business plan, the recipient acknowledges and agrees that: (i) in the event the recipient does not wish to pursue this matter, the recipient will return this copy to the address listed below as soon as practical; (ii) the recipient will not copy, fax, reproduce, or distribute this confidential business plan, in whole or in part, without permission; and (iii) all of the information contained herein will be treated as confidential material.

CONTROLLED COPY
Issued to: _____
Issue Date: _____
Copy No. _____

For Information Contact:
Crazed Consultant
Crazed Consultant Films Int'l.
Street Address City, State
Phone

1/EXECUTIVE SUMMARY

Strategic Opportunity

- The U.S. box office reached $9.5 billion in 2002, up from $8.4 billion in 2001.
- The U.S. box office for independent films in 2002 was $3.4 billion.
- The worldwide revenues for U.S. independent films is estimated at $7 billion.
- Global boxoffice revenues in 2002 were $19.1 billion.

Crazed Consultant Films International (CCFI) is a start-up enterprise engaged in the development and production of motion picture films for theatrical release. CCFI's goals are to make films that will raise the consciousness of the American public about the importance of household cats, and that will be commercially exploitable to a mass audience. The Company plans to produce three films over the next five years, with budgets ranging from $500,000 to $10 million.

Management Team

At the core of CCFI are the founders, who bring to the Company successful entrepreneurial experience and in-depth expertise in motion picture production. The team is complemented by a support group of consultants and advisers.

The Product

CCFI owns options on Jane Lovable's first three Leonard the Wonder Cat books and has first refusal on the next three publications. Currently, one book is in print, another is about to be published, and a third is still in the writing stage. The first book has created an established audience for the films.

The movies, based on Lovable's series, will star Leonard, a half-Siamese, half-mongrel cat, whose adventures make for entertaining stories that incorporate a strong moral lesson. CCFI expects each film to stand on its own and to produce profits to finance each successive film. The movies are designed to capture the interest of the entire family, building significantly on an already established base.

The Industry

The successes of *My Big Fat Greek Wedding* in 2002, which has earned more than $240 million to-date domestically, and 1999's low-budget film *The Blair Witch Project*, which earned more than $300 million in worldwide revenues, have revolutionized how studios and distributors look at the production and marketing of films. Independent films can vary widely in budget, from as low as $30,000 to as high as $100 million, but their similarities are the freedom to be in control creatively and from the homogeneity of studio production. By definition, an independent film is one that is financed by any source other than a U.S. studio. With their ability to take more time and their need to plan budgets more carefully than studios tend to do with their big-budget films, smaller companies are able to give greater attention to their lower-budgeted, intelligent dramas. Unlike studios, the independent production companies are able to avoid substantial overhead.

The Market

Family films with sophisticated and updated storylines have been making a comeback at the box office. The public is ready for mainstream films that present feline themes. The commercial success in recent years of animal films, such as *Cats and Dogs, Dr. Dolittle* and *Dr. Dolittle 2*, have opened the door for cat films. As the pet that is owned by more individuals than any other animal in the U.S., the cat will draw audiences from far and wide.

It has historically been true that in hard economic times, family entertainment wins out. People want to be entertained and forget their troubles. We feel that films that offer diversion and feature a strong cat story line will draw a large audience.

Heretofore, the majority of family films have been made by studios. We believe that the time is right to make cost-effective films on smaller budgets. Once the cat genre has become popular, our films will be able to move into large commercial theaters. Crazed Consultant Films International plans to keep its films independent in order to maintain the quality of the story and the filming.

Distribution

The Company will seek distribution by independent companies whose proven ability to handle low-budget films with sensitive themes appeals to CCFI's desire for special handling. We will hold screenings in Los Angeles and/or New York specifically for companies who have experience with the family film genre. In addition, we will take the films to markets and film festivals where appropriate.

The foreign markets have become more profitable for family films in the past few years. As our reputation for quality films grows, both domestic and foreign markets will be anxious to buy our product. CCFI expects to establish a brand which will allow the company to have increasing leverage over the next few years in negotiating deals and attracting major cast and directorial elements.

Investment Opportunity and Financial Highlights

The founders are seeking an equity investment of approximately $15 million for production of three films and overhead expenditures. Current projections indicate a pretax net profit of $55.7 million on the initial investment for all three films. CCFI will also entertain proposals to make one film at a time and roll those profits over into the subsequent films.

2/THE COMPANY

Crazed Consultant Films International is a privately-owned California corporation that was established in September 1999. Our principal purpose and business is to create theatrical motion pictures. The Company plans to develop and produce quality family-themed films portraying positive images of the household cat.

The public is ready for films with feline themes. Big budget animal-themed films have opened the market over the last five years. In addition, the changing balance of cat over dog owners is an allegory for changes in society overall. The objectives of CCFI are as follows:

1. To produce quality films that provide positive family entertainment with moral tales designed for both enjoyment and education.

2. To make films that will celebrate the importance of the household cat and that will be exploitable to a mass audience.
3. To produce three feature films in the first five years, with budgets ranging from $500,000 to $10 million.
4. To develop scripts with outside writers.
5. To explore overseas co-production and co-financing potential for the Company.
6. To distribute our films through independent distribution companies.

There is a need and a hunger for more family films. We believe that we can make exciting films starting as low as $500,000 without sacrificing quality. Until recently, there was a dearth of cat films. Far more attention has been paid to dogs, who are alleged to be "man's best friend." However, the emergence of cats as the most popular pet in the United States has changed that picture. Cats are at least woman's best friend, and women often drive the box office.

We plan to change the emphasis of movies from pigs and dogs to cats, while providing meaningful and wholesome entertainment that will attract the entire family. In view of the growth of the family market in the last few years, the cat theme is one that has been undervalued and, consequently, underexploited. Part of the growth has been due to the historical success of "feel-good" films during economic downturns; in addition, there has been a general worldwide emphasis on returning to traditional family values. For these reasons, animal films with sophisticated and modern story lines have been making a comeback at the box office and appeal to moviegoers of all ages.

CCFI's films will feature Leonard, hero of Jane Lovable's Leonard the Wonder Cat books. The Company perceives a large, presold audience. The first book in the series has sold 10 million copies not only to children and preteens but teenagers and adults as well.

Management and Organization

The primary strength of any company is in its management team. CCFI's principals, Ms. Lotta Mogul and Mr. Gimme Bucks, have extensive experience in business and in the entertainment industry. In addition, the Company has relationships with key consultants and advisers who will be available to fill important roles on an as-needed basis. The following individuals make up the current management team and key managers:

Ms. Lotta Mogul, President and Executive Producer

Lotta Mogul spent three years at Jeffcarl Studios as a producer. Among her many credits are *Lord of the Litter Box, The Dog Who Came for Dinner,* and *Fluffy and Fido Go to College.* These films all had budgets under $10 million and had combined grosses of more than $600 million worldwide. As President and Executive Producer, her considerable experience will be used to create our production slate, manage the CCFI team, negotiate with distributors, and plan future strategies.

Mr. Gimme Bucks, Vice-President, Financial Affairs

Gimme Bucks will oversee the long-term strategy and financial affairs of the company. A graduate of the University of California at Los Angeles, Bucks has an M.B.A. He worked in business affairs at XYZ Studios and has been a consultant to small, independent film companies.

Mr. Better Focus, Cinematographer

Better Focus is a member of the American Society of Cinematographers. He was Alpha Numerical's director of photography for several years. He won an Emmy Award for his work on *Unusual Birds of Ottumwa,* and he has been nominated twice for Academy Awards.

Ms. Ladder Climber, Production and Development

Ladder Climber will assist in the production of our films. She began her career as an assistant to the producer of the cult film *Dogs That Bark* and has worked her way up to production manager and line producer on several films. Most recently, she served as line producer on *The Paw* and *Thirty Miles to Azusa.*

Consultants

We plan to hire producers for individual projects as required by the production schedule. The office staff will be lean but will expand as the work load demands. In the meantime, we are also working with the following consultants:

Samuel Torts, Attorney-at-Law, Los Angeles, CA
Winners and Losers, Certified Public Accountants,
    Los Angeles, CA.

3/FILM PROJECTS

CCFI currently controls the rights to the first three Leonard the Wonder Cat books, which will be the basis for its film projects over the next five years. In March 2002, the Company paid $10,000 for three-year options on the first three books with first refusal on the next three. The author will receive additional payments over the next four years as production begins. The Leonard series, written by Jane Lovable, has been obtained at very inexpensive option prices due to the author's respect for Ms. Mogul's devotion to charitable cat causes. Three film projects are scheduled.

Leonard's Love

The first film will be based on the novel *Leonard's Love*, which has sold 10 million copies. The story revolves around the friendship between a girl, Natasha, and her cat, Leonard. The two leave the big city to live in a small town, where they discover the true meaning of life.

Furry Catman has written the screenplay. The projected budget for *Leonard's Love* is $500,000, with CCFI producing and Ultra Virtuoso directing. Virtuoso's previous credits include a low-budget feature, *My Life as a Ferret*, and two rock videos, *Feral Love* and *Hot Fluffy Rag*. We are currently in the development stage with this project. The initial script has been written, but we have no commitments from actors. Casting will commence once financing is in place. As a marketing plus, the upcoming movie will be advertised on the cover of the new paperback edition of the book.

Len's Big Thrill

This film is based on the second Leonard book, which is currently in the prepublication stage. In the story, Leonard goes with

Natasha while she auditions for a movie role. When Len struts across the room, the director—Simon Sez—is captivated by Len's natural ease in front of a camera. Simon makes a deal for both Natasha and Leonard to be in the film, rewriting the script to feature Leonard as the cat who saves his mistress from a burning building. The film is a smash with audiences and two sequels are made. Finally realizing they are in love, Natasha and Simon marry giving Len the biggest thrill of all.

Ultra Virtuoso is set to direct this feature also. Development on this project will start after we are in production on *Leonard's Love*. Current estimates place the budget at $2.5 million. We plan to interview screenwriters as soon as the shooting script for the first film is finalized.

Cat Follies

The third book in the series is currently being written by Ms. Lovable and will be published in late 2004. The story features a dejected Leonard, whose films aren't drawing the audiences they used to. No matter what Natasha and Simon, his human parents, try, they can't cheer up our cat. Desperate to find something to encourage Len, they take him for ice skating lessons. Amazed at Leonard's agility on skates, his teacher contacts the Wonderland Follies, who sign Leonard to a contract. He is an immediate hit with the audience, especially the young people. As luck would have it, one night film mogul Harvey Hoffenbrauer is in the audience. Seeing the reaction of both kids and adults to Leonard, he decides to make a film of the follies. Soon Leonard is back on top.

4/THE INDUSTRY

Along with many corporations in the United States, the major studios began the radical process of restructuring or "downsizing" at the end of the 1990s. While in the past they all maintained expensive production facilities and staff and significant overhead expenses, the impact of unions and guilds and runaway productions forced studios to follow new business models. Those companies are releasing fewer films but expect greater grosses per film. As a consequence, smaller production companies with lower-budgeted films have been able to command a bigger share of the market. *The Blair Witch Project* and *My Big Fat Greek Wedding* are two examples of smaller films that have scored high grosses. The success of these and other low-budget films have hastened a change in the structure of the industry with all of the studios creating or planning to have specialty divisions.

The 2002 box office for independent films accounted for $3.4 billion of North American boxoffice receipts, 36 percent of the total $9.5 billion total box office. In addition, the most recent annual survey of the American Film Marketing Association (AFMA) of overseas sales shows a total of $2.6 billion for U.S. independent films. When the AFMA total is added to U.S. box office, along with U.S. ancillary revenues (estimated at more than $1 billion), the worldwide market for U.S. independent films is estimated at more than $7 billion. Independent films, by definition, are those financed by any source other than a U.S. studio.

Studios and distributors look at the production and marketing of films. Independent films can vary widely in budget, from as low as $30,000 to as high as $100 million, but their similarity is a freedom from the homogeneity of studio production. With their ability to take more time and their need to plan budgets more carefully than studios with deep pockets tend to do with their big-budget films, smaller companies are able to give greater attention to their lower-budgeted, intelligent dramas. Unlike studios, the independent production companies are able to avoid substantial overhead costs by hiring creative and other production personnel on a project-by-project basis. And due to their lower budgets, these films can be directed at niche markets rather than needing to appeal to the entire body of the filmgoing audience. They typically finance their production activities from discrete sources, and their goal is to completely finance their motion pictures before the commencement of principal photography.

Baskerville Communications of the U.K. has forecasted global boxoffice revenues to grow to $28 billion by 2010. Together, China, the United States, and India account for 67 percent of the global screen count. Ten countries house about 80 percent of the world's screens. In his annual report, Jack Valenti, head of the Motion Picture Association of America (MPAA), reported that 1.64 billion tickets were sold in 2002, "an expansion of 10.2 percent over 2001, the largest admissions increase in the past 45 years, in that long-ago time when Dwight Eisenhower was President." While U.S. theatrical distribution is still the first choice of any feature-length film, international markets are gaining even greater strength than they had before. U.S. feature film distributors are projected to raise their total worldwide revenue windows to $31 billion by 2010.

At a studio, a film begins in one of two ways. Someone inside the company might develop a "concept" (one or two lines of an idea), or a known writer might make the well-known "30-second pitch" and secure a deal. On the other hand, an agent might bring a script by a new writer to the attention of the studio. Scriptwriters are hired, lead actors sought, budgets approved, and directors and producers assigned. This process is called "development."

The next step is "preproduction," the period before principal photography when commitments are sought for talent, budgets are finalized, the director and crew are hired, and most of the contracts are negotiated and signed. Producers try to have all contracts in place before filming begins; however, sometimes stars don't sign until after the filming has started. The filming of a motion picture is called "principal photography." It takes from eight to 12 weeks, although major cast members may not be used for the entire period. Once the production has gotten to this stage, it is unlikely that a studio will shut it down unless there are "creative differences" with a star or director. Even if the picture goes over the budget, the studio will usually find a way to complete it.

During the post-production period that follows principal photography, the film is edited and synchronized with music and dialogue. In certain cases, special effects are added. The post-production period used to require six to nine months. With recent technological developments, however, this time has been cut drastically for some films.

Theatrical Exhibition

The exhibitor pays a percentage of the picture's boxoffice receipts (called "rentals") to the studio or distributor. The size of this split depends on the distributor's strength and the exhibitor's desire to show the film. While the split for independent films may be 48 or 49 percent of the total, the database generally shows that both the studio and independent distributor receive a 50/50 split. Of course, the exhibitor keeps all the money for popcorn, candy, and soft drinks.

Major studio films may go out to as many as 3,000 screens in the first few weeks. Independent films start more slowly and build on their success. An independent film may open on as few as one screen or as many as 500. Although the amount of rentals will decline toward the end of the film's run, it may very well increase in the first few months. It is not unusual for a smaller film to gain theaters as it becomes more popular.

Because revenues from all other sources are driven by the success of the theatrical distribution, a film's stay on theater screens is important. Coupled with this is the exhibitor's basic desire to see people sitting in theater seats. Although the studio has some power to keep a mediocre film on the screen with its greater resources for marketing and promotion, good independent films will be shown. Exhibitors have always maintained that they will show any film they think their customers will pay to see. Depending on the location of the individual theater or the chain, local pressures may play a part in deciding which films are shown. Not all pictures are appropriate for all theaters. Despite the new technologies on the horizon, theatrical exhibition is not likely to disappear during our lifetime.

OTHER SOURCES OF REVENUE

Cable and Broadcast Television

Television exhibition includes over-the-air reception for viewers either through a fee system (cable) or "free television" (national and independent broadcast stations). The proliferation of new cable networks in the last 15 years has made cable (both basic and premium stations) one of the most important outlets for feature films and documentaries. Whereas network and independent television stations were a substantial part of the revenue picture in the seventies and early eighties, cable has become a far more important ancillary outlet. The pay-per-view (PPV) business has continued to grow, thanks to continued DBS (direct broadcast satellite) growth and significant NVOD (near video on demand) rollouts by cable operators. Pay-per-view and pay television allow cable television subscribers to purchase individual films or special events or subscribe to premium cable channels for a fee. Both acquire their film programming by purchasing the distribution rights from motion picture distributors.

Home Video/DVD

A large source of motion picture revenues continues to be the worldwide home video market. Home video companies promote and sell videocassettes and videodiscs to local, regional, and national video retailers, which then rent the cassettes and discs to consumers for private viewing. While DVD use is growing, VHS rentals are expected to remain a major source of home entertainment income in the near future. Trade groups put spending on the rental and purchase of videocassettes and DVDs at $16.9 billion in 2001, up 21 percent from $13.9 billion in 2000.

International Theatrical and Ancillaries

Much of the projected growth in the worldwide film business comes from the international markets. Distributors and exhibitors keep finding new ways to increase the boxoffice revenue pool. The growth in multiplexes in Europe has been followed by more screens in Asia and Latin America, but this growth has slowed. The world screen count is predicted to remain static over the next nine years at 149,000, as several territories shed traditional theaters. Other factors are the privatization of television stations overseas, the introduction of direct broadcast satellite services and increased cable penetration.

Future Trends

New technologies are volatile in their movements and can change at any time. DVD, for example, which came into the American market later than expected due to problems with determining standards, is now supported by all the major studios. Globally, 26 million households will be capable of accessing video-on-demand (VOD) services by 2005, with the vast majority—83 percent—in the U.S. According to *Screen Digest*, 22 percent of U.S. television households will have access to VOD by 2005, while the United Kingdom will lead the way in Europe. A digital feature film projection and distribution system is five to 10 years away.

5/THE MARKET

An independent film goes through the same process from development and preproduction through production and post-production as a studio film. In this case, however, development and preproduction may involve only one or two people. And the entrepreneur, whether producer or director, maintains control over the final product. An independent company is one that finds its production financing outside of the studios. An independent film may be distributed by a studio, but its negative cost has been found from other sources. Many of the large production companies started with the success of a single film. Carolco was built on the success of *Rambo III* and *Terminator II*; New Line achieved prominence and clout with the *Nightmare on Elm Street* series.

The smaller production company usually raises money for one film at a time, although there may be other films in different phases of development. Many companies are owned or controlled by the creative person, such as a writer/director or writer/producer, in combination with a financial partner or group. As small companies go out of business, new ones form to take their place. Since the beginning of the 1990s, independent film has been going through one of its "up" cycles. Traditionally, the fortunes of independent filmmakers have always varied from year to year. The recent success of independent films has sent the independent segment into another growth spurt.

The market for specialty films has also been growing. All across the United States are individual, independently-owned theaters that maintain their own direct mail lists of faithful moviegoers. Often, a film made for $500,000 or less can earn back its costs from these regulars alone. Until recently, the independently-owned theaters were thought of as the home of the offbeat and unique film.

Crazed Consultant Films International feels that its first film will create a new type of moviegoer for these theaters and a new type of commercial film for the mainstream theaters. Just as *My Dog Skip* found a home in both art houses and malls, so will *Leonard's Love*. Although we expect our film to have a universal enough appeal to play in the mainstream houses, at its projected budget it may begin in the specialty theaters.

Because of the low budget, exhibitors may wait for our first film to prove itself before providing access to screens in the larger movie houses. In addition, smaller houses will give us a chance to expand the film on a slow basis and build awareness with the public. As word of mouth increases, both the distributor and the owners of the big theater chains will want to have the Leonard films in the mall theaters.

Although the Company will be making films about a cat, the themes are intended to be typical genres that will appeal to a mass audience. The stories will cover romance, mystery, coming of age, and other generally popular subjects. We feel that the time has finally come for the cat genre film. Cats have been with us for 12 million years, but they have been under-appreciated and under-exploited, especially by Hollywood. Historically, cats have had their ups and downs. Early societies revered the cat, but later on, cats, especially black ones, were categorized with witches and burned at the stake. The motion picture industry has exploited only this latter view, often casting cats as killers or as attached in some way to the supernatural in films such as *Stuart Little* and *Cats and Dogs*.

Recent studies have shown that the cat has become the pet of choice. The tremendous success of canine films has only increased the window of opportunity for our films. Stephen King's *Sleepwalkers*, in which cats save the heroine by attacking supernatural beings, was a beginning. However, we plan to present cats in their true light as regular, everyday heroes with all the lightness and gaiety of other current animal cinema favorites, including dogs, horses, pigs, and bears. In following the tradition of the dog film genre, we are also looking down the road to cable outlets. We believe that cat programs will be the next trend in this medium. There is even talk of a cat channel. CCFI plans to begin with a $500,000 film that would benefit from exposure through the film festival circuit. The exposure of our films at festivals and limited runs in specialty theaters in target areas will create an awareness for them with the general public. In addition, we plan to tie in sales of the Leonard books with the films.

Although a major studio would be a natural place to go with these films, we want to remain independent. The niche market is strong enough to support the Company as an independent producer. Many dog films, such as *Beethoven*, *Bingo*, and *K-9*, have been made by major studios with significant budgets. *My Dog Skip* and *Air Bud* were independent films with budgets reportedly under $7 million. We can make a good film at a lower budget that will attract the same audiences.

Competitive Advantages

Crazed Consultant Films International has several market advantages:

1. The two principals have experience in both the creative and business areas of motion pictures. Ms. Lotta Mogul

has significant production company experience.
Mr. Gimme Bucks is well-versed in the independent
finance arena.

2. The company is run by people who are devoted to the idea
   of presenting the Leonard stories in a cost-effective but
   entertaining fashion. Their devotion to quality will create
   low-budget films with much higher values on the screen
   than their budgets would dictate.

3. CCFI controls the rights to specific books, the first of which
   has sold well in publication. The commercial tie-in of
   a book with its ready-made market of readers is important
   to distributors. It gives them the all-important "hook" for
   publicizing the film.

4. Management commits to promote the films wherever
   and whenever possible. Promotional appearances, tours,
   and interviews involving a picture's actors, director, and
   writers are often critical for gaining the attention and
   acceptance for an independent film in today's competitive
   marketplace.

6/DISTRIBUTION

Most of the marketing strategies commonly employed by independent distributors will be used to market CCFI's films. The actual marketing of the film itself is the distributor's job. It involves the representation of the film in terms of genre, the placement of advertisements in various media, the selection of a sales approach for exhibitors and foreign buyers, and the "hype" (word of mouth, promotional events, alliances with special interest groups, and so on). All of these factors are critical to a film's success.

Each major studio has its own distribution division. All marketing and other distribution decisions are made in-house. This division sends out promotional and advertising materials, arranges screenings of films, and makes deals with domestic and foreign distributors. The studios each release 15 to 25 films a year, and they occasionally acquire independent films to release. For our films, however, we will seek distribution by an independent company.

We feel that independent distributors often have the knowledge and patience to give special care to eclectic or mixed-genre films. Many independents will allow a film to find its audience slowly and methodically. However, this does not mean that independent distributors will not want to release films with mass appeal. For such films with smaller budgets and lesser names, independents often have an expertise that the studios lack. In addition, by focusing their marketing and promotional efforts on a handful of primary markets, these companies are able to keep their costs relatively low. Because their focus is on fewer films, we feel that our films will receive better care than at a studio.

The first step in distributing a film is having copies made of it for motion picture presentation. The prints sent to the theaters are duplications of the "master" print, which is made from the original edited negative. A print usually costs $1,200 to $1,500, depending on the length of the film and current film stock costs. Major studio films typically are opened wide—that is, on thousands of screens simultaneously. The cost of prints for that type of release is more than $1 million, which is impossible for low-budget films. Although the independent distributor begins with fewer prints, several hundred may be made throughout the film's release period. While a film is in release, therefore, the total print cost can be appreciable.

The domestic territory is defined as both the United States and Canada combined. Many of the independent distributors consider the United States and Canada to be one package and prefer not to have them separated beforehand. Domestic rights refer not only to theatrical distribution but to all other media, such as video, cable, pay-per-view, and television. When a producer secures an advance from one of these media for production financing, he or she makes the deal a little less attractive to potential distributors by fractionalizing the rights. Any source of future revenue that is taken out of the potential money pie makes it more difficult for the producer to close the distribution deal.

In terms of foreign sales, there are U.S.-based distributors who specialize in the rest of the world. These companies deal with networks of subdistributors in various countries. It is important to distinguish between a distributor and a foreign sales agent. If a distribution company is granted the rights to the film for the foreign markets, that company is the distributor. Generally, if the ownership of the foreign rights is retained by the producer, who grants someone only a percentage of the receipts in exchange for obtaining distribution contracts in each territory or for various media throughout the world, that person is actually a sales agent.

There is no typical distribution deal. The distribution company will take as much as it can get. It is CCFI's job to give away as little as possible. Based on industry averages, we have used a distributor fee of 34 percent of the total revenue in our projections. These percentages apply only to the revenues generated by the distributor's deals; if that company is only making foreign sales, then it takes a percentage of only foreign revenues. How much the distribution company wants depends on its participation in the entire film package. The greater the up-front expense that the company must assume, the greater the percentage of incoming revenues it will seek.

In acquiring a project, the distributor looks at the following elements, among others:

- Uniqueness of storyline
- Special audience segment for the type or genre of film
- Ability of the cast members to attract audiences or buyers on their names alone
- Past successes of the producers and/or director
- Name tie-in from another medium; for example, a best-selling novel
- Attached money

Our films will meet these criteria easily. Necessary to selling a film is a mix of elements, although the story is always the first concern. The exhibitors to whom the distributor sells must see something in the film that they can promote to their audiences. This changes from country to country and depends on the perspective of the buyer.

Release Strategies

The ways in which a film is distributed domestically (in the United States and Canada) vary with the size of the distribution company and the type of film. Audience segmentation is determined by critical appraisal and the likely interest that the film will generate. For example, the distributor might release a film carefully, market by market, and use revenues from the first group of theaters to finance the prints and advertising for the second group, and so on.

Independent distributors use several standard patterns of release strategies. The usual method is to release a film on a few screens at a time and slowly take it to more screens. A popular film may well end up in large multiplexes—but usually after the film has been out for a while. This method has two advantages. It allows unique films to receive special handling, and it allows a popular-genre, low-budget film to move as fast as its advertising budget permits.

"Saturation," "platform," "rollout," and "sequencing" releases are variations on this theme. The film opens on a few selected screens and moves to others throughout the country in some sort of pattern. A particular film might work best in one market because of the makeup of the population, because the film was shot there, or because residents will go to see almost anything. With good reviews, a film will continue to move through the country in one of several fashions. It might move to contiguous states, open on successive screens based on a certain time pattern, or cascade into the markets that are expected to produce the highest revenue. Whatever method is used, the film continues to open on more and more screens. Eventually, the number of screens will decline, but the film will remain in distribution as long as it continues to attract audiences. The plan for CCFI's first film is to realize sizable opening audiences (relative to the budget and theme of the film) and good reviews, then use the money and reviews to continue releasing the film on additional screens. Clearly, no one expects a $500,000 film to sell $17 or $20 million in tickets during its first weekend—or at all. The distributor will fund the copying of more prints out of the revenues from the first couple of theaters. Advertising will work in the same way. Ads in a major city newspaper can cost anywhere between $1,000 and $10,000. As a low or moderate-budget film earns money, it finances the advertising in the cities in which it will open later.

A very small company may use another method of distribution: "90/10" deals are actually booking procedures that go hand-in-hand with the release of small films. The distributor makes a deal with the theater to put up 90 percent of the advertising money and take 90 percent of the gross, after the exhibitor takes an agreed-upon minimum guarantee to earn the house "nut." This type of deal could be done at other percentages, but 90/10 is common. The type of distributor that we hope to attract will probably use this procedure for our first film. As we move to the $2.5 million budget level, and certainly at the $10 million level, we will be able to move out of the specialty arena and into more chain theaters.

7/RISK STATEMENT

Investment in the film industry is highly speculative and inherently risky. There can be no assurance of the economic success of any motion picture since the revenues derived from the production and distribution of a motion picture depend primarily upon its acceptance by the public, which cannot be predicted. The commercial success of a motion picture also depends upon the quality and acceptance of other competing films released into the marketplace at or near the same time, general economic factors and other tangible and intangible factors, all of which can change and cannot be predicted with certainty.

The entertainment industry in general, and the motion picture industry in particular, are continuing to undergo significant changes, primarily due to technological developments. Although these developments have resulted in the availability of alternative and competing forms of leisure time entertainment, such technological developments have also resulted in the creation of additional revenue sources through licensing of rights to such new media, and potentially could lead to future reductions in the costs of producing and distributing motion pictures. In addition, the theatrical success of a motion picture remains a crucial factor in generating revenues in other media such as videocassettes and television. Due to the rapid growth of technology, shifting consumer tastes, and the popularity and availability of other forms of entertainment, it is impossible to predict the overall effect these factors will have on the potential revenue from and profitability of feature-length motion pictures.

The Company itself is in the organizational stage and is subject to all the risks incident to the creation and development of a new business, including the absence of a history of operations and minimal net worth. In order to prosper, the success of CCFI will depend partly upon the ability of management to produce a film of exceptional quality at a lower cost which can compete in appeal with higher-budgeted films of the same genre. In order to minimize this risk, management plans to participate as much as possible throughout the process and will aim to mitigate financial risks where possible. Fulfilling this goal depends on the timing of investor financing, the ability to obtain distribution contracts with satisfactory terms and the continued participation of the current management.

8/FINANCING

The financial projections for CCFI assume a conservative level of success for each film project. Many factors affect the success of any film project, including the following:

- Innate commercial appeal
- Casting
- Direction
- Timing of release
- Distribution patterns

A film's commercial appeal is undoubtedly the single most significant factor in determining its financial success. This is closely followed in importance by the agreement that the production company has with its film distributors. However, all of these factors affect the eventual bottom line.

For the purposes of this business plan, we have used current industry results for independent films of comparable size and theme. Since there have not been significant cat films, we have used canine films as a guide. In addition, we looked at typical independent films in the budget ranges of our proposed projects.

Any film that is a "breakout"—that is, a critical and boxoffice hit—will be over and above the financials we show. We have not factored the blockbuster low-budget films into our numbers, as they would skew our results to the high side, causing unrealistic expectations. Should one of our films earn above-average dollars, it will increase the projected revenues, putting us ahead of our anticipated profit levels. Although the print and advertising expenditures may increase at the same time, their amount is expected to be minimal compared to the additional revenues.

To help protect CCFI and the Company's investors from losses, CCFI will endeavor to secure presale, distribution, and other financing agreements. Given that this company is new, an agreement will be entered into only if it is perceived to benefit all equity investors. In a presale agreement, a foreign organization or person buys the ancillary rights (domestic or foreign) in advance. The filmmaker takes this commitment, which includes a guarantee to pay a specific amount upon delivery of the completed film, to one of several specialized entertainment banks and, if the bank accepts the commitment, is able to raise money to finance production. In exchange for the presale contract, the U.S. or foreign buyer obtains the right to keep the revenue (rentals) from a particular territory and may also seek equity participation. The agreement can be for a certain length of time, a revenue cap, or both.

The Financing Plan

This section contains CCFI's sales projections and income statements for the five years beginning with production financing. The projections are based on the history of other films as well as current trends in the industry. The following are significant elements of our forecast.

Financial Assumptions

For the purposes of the business plan, several assumptions have been included in the financial scenarios and are noted accordingly:

1. **Box Office** reflects gross dollars of ticket sales before the exhibitor splits the total with the distributor. **Domestic Rentals** reflect the distributor's share of the box office split with the exhibitor in the United States and Canada, assuming the film has the same distributor in both . countries. **Domestic Other** (also known as "ancillary") includes home video, cable, network television, and television syndication. **Foreign Revenue** includes all monies returned to distributors from all venues outside the United States and Canada.
2. All funds flow from each revenue source to the distributor, whose expenses are deducted before any money goes to the producer/investor; therefore, gross profit is shown as the **Distributor's Gross Profit**. This is the income before the distributor takes his fee. Depending on negotiations, after the distributor deducts the costs for prints and ads, the investor generally is paid back the budget cost. Then the distributor deducts his fees. The timing of disbursements, however, is always subject to negotiation.
3. The **Budget**, also known as the film's "negative costs," covers only the expenses that are needed to create the master print of each film. All marketing costs are included under **P&A** (Prints and Advertising), often referred to as

"releasing costs" or "distribution expenses." These expenses also include the cost of making copies of the print from the master and advertising.

4. The films shown in Tables 1 through 4 are used as the basis for the projections. The rationale for the projections is explained in number (9) below. The films relate either in feeling or budget to our three films. It should be noted that these groups do not include films whose results are known but that have lost money. In addition, there are no databases that collect all the films ever made, nor are budgets available for all films released. There is, therefore, a built-in bias in the data used.

5. Table 1, "**Gross Profits Of Selected Films With Varied Genres With Budgets $600,000 to $5 Million, Years 1999–2001**," shows gross profit results for films before distributor fees have been deducted.

6. Table 2, "**Selected Films With Varied Genres North American Box Office And Budgets Only With Budgets of $200,000 to $5 Million, Years 2002–2003**," shows gross income results for films with comparative budgets in the last two years. Due to the two-year time span in the return from ancillary and foreign venues, the worldwide income from these films is not known at this time.

7. Table 3, "**Gross Profits Of Selected Films With Varied Genres With Budgets Of $5.5 to $20 Million, Years 2002–2003**," shows gross profit results for films before distributor fees have been deducted.

8. Table 4, "**Selected Films With Varied Genres North American Box Office and Budgets Only With Budgets $6 to $20 Million**" shows gross income results for films with comparative budgets in the last two years. Due to the two-year time span in the return from ancillary and foreign venues, the worldwide income from these films is not known at this time.

9. Table 5 shows the projected income statement for the three films. The revenue scenarios are moderate projections based on the data shown in Tables 1 through 4. They are used for the cash flows in Table 6. Due to the wide variance in the results of individual films, simple averages of actual data are not realistic. Each element in the forecasts has been calculated as a percentage of either

the budget (box office and prints and ads) or the box office (all other revenues). In this way, films of different budgets can be compared to one another without too much skewing of the data. The box office is calculated first as a percentage of the budget. Then the rest of the revenues are calculated as a percentage of box office. The cost of prints and ads (P&A) is then calculated as a percentage of the budget. In order to keep uncommonly high or low results from affecting the projections, the high and low results in each individual revenue and cost category have been discarded in observing the data.

10. **Distributor's Fees** (the distributor's share of the revenues as compared to his expenses, which represent out-of-pocket costs) are based on 35 percent of all distributor gross revenue (note: the exhibition portion is separate from this calculation), both domestic and foreign.

11. **Net Producer/Investor Income** represents the projected pre-tax profit after the distributor's expenses and fees have been deducted and prior to negotiated distributions to investors.

12. The cash flow assumptions for Table 6 are:
    a) Film production will take one year from development through post-production, ending with the creation of a master print. The actual release date depends on finalization of distribution arrangements, which may occur either before or after the film has been completed and is an unknown variable at this time. For purposes of the cash flow, we have assumed distribution will start within six months after completion of the film.
    b) The largest portion of print and advertising costs will be spent in the first quarter of the film's opening.
    c) The majority of revenues will come back to the producers within two years after release of the film, although a smaller amount of ancillary revenues will take longer to occur and will be covered by the investor's agreement.

13. Due to the timing of the cash requirements needed to produce the films, draw downs not immediately used will be deposited in an interest-bearing account.

TABLE 10.1
CRAZED CONSULTANT FILMS INTERNATIONAL
GROSS PROFITS OF SELECTED FILMS WITH VARIED GENRES
WITH BUDGETS OF $400,000 TO $5 MILLION
YEARS 1999–2001
(Millions of Dollars)

FILMS	DOMESTIC REVENUE			FOREIGN REVENUE (c)	TOTAL REVENUE (d)	COSTS			DISTRIBUTOR'S GROSS PROFIT (e)
	BOX OFFICE	RENTALS (a)	OTHER (b)			BUDGET	P&A	TOTAL	
1999									
Catch The Catnip	9.0	4.5	11.0	13.0	28.5	3.0	7.0	10.0	18.5
Digging For Bones	18.0	9.0	14.5	30.0	53.5	4.5	17.5	22	31.5
Fluffy The Lap Dancer	6.8	3.4	10.5	7.0	20.9	0.7	4.0	4.7	16.2
French Poodle Diaries	6.4	3.2	6.5	5.7	15.4	1.5	2.9	4.4	11.0
2000									
Hairball Heaven	12.0	6.0	18.0	10.0	34.0	4.0	15.0	19.0	15.0
Kibble Hunter	15.4	7.7	20.0	18.0	45.7	5.0	9.8	14.8	30.9
Buffy of Sherman Oaks	4.0	2.0	8.0	7.0	17.0	0.4	3.0	3.4	13.6
Snowball's Last Love	10.0	5.0	6.7	8.0	19.7	3.0	4.5	7.5	12.2
2001									
Lord of the Litter Box	15.4	7.7	28.0	27.0	62.7	5.0	9.8	14.8	47.9
Manx Marauders	6.0	3.0	10.0	7.0	20.0	0.5	6.0	6.5	13.5
My Big Fat Siamese	13.8	6.7	35.0	25.0	66.7	3.8	6.6	10.4	56.3
Precinct Tabby	20.7	10.4	21.2	15.4	47.0	5.0	15.0	20.0	27.0
Witch Of Blair Street	5.0	2.5	9.0	3.5	15.0	0.5	2.1	2.6	12.4

(a) Rentals equal distributor's share of U.S. box office.
(b) Domestic Other Revenue includes television, cable, video, and all other non-theatrical sources of revenue.
(c) Foreign Revenue includes both theatrical and ancillary revenues.
(d) Total Revenue equals Domestic Rentals, Domestic Other, and Foreign.
(e) Gross Profit before distributor's fee is removed.

Source: Business Strategies.

© Copyright 2003 Crazed Consultant Films International

TABLE 10.2
CRAZED CONSULTANT FILMS INTERNATIONAL
SELECTED FILMS WITH VARIED GENRES
U.S. BOX OFFICE AND BUDGETS ONLY
WITH BUDGETS OF $200,000 TO $5 MILLION
YEARS 2002–2003
(Millions of Dollars)

FILM	BOX OFFICE	BUDGET
Film 1	15.0	4.0
Film 2	12.8	2.0
Film 3	6.9	1.5
Film 4	6.8	5.0
Film 5	9.8	0.2
Film 6	14.6	3.5
Film 7	10.8	4.5
Film 8	24.0	5.0
Film 9	12.5	3.0
Film 10	7.0	2.0
Film 11	12.2	3.3
Film 12	4.3	1.5

Note: Domestic ancillary and all foreign data generally are not available until two years after a film's initial U.S. release.

Source: Business Strategies.

© Copyright 2003 Crazed Consultant Films International

TABLE 10.3
CRAZED CONSULTANT FILMS INTERNATIONAL
GROSS PROFITS OF SELECTED FILMS WITH VARIED GENRES
WITH BUDGETS OF $5.5 TO $20 MILLION
YEARS 2002–2003
(Millions of Dollars)

FILMS	DOMESTIC REVENUE			FOREIGN REVENUE(c)	TOTAL REVENUE(d)	COSTS			DISTRIBUTOR'S GROSS PROFIT (e)
	BOX OFFICE	RENTALS(a)	OTHER(b)			BUDGET	P&A	TOTAL	
1999									
Beaver Ball	45.0	15.0	60.0	60.0	135.0	15.0	25.0	40.0	95.0
Cat-A-Tonic	15.0	7.5	35.0	24.0	66.5	7.0	9.0	16.0	50.5
Cincinnati Bear	20.0	10.0	25.0	18.0	53.0	8.4	10.0	18.4	34.6
Fluffy In Space	10.0	5.0	11.0	12.0	28.0	5.5	6.0	11.5	16.5
2000									
German Shepherd In Space	28.0	14.0	45.0	18.0	77.0	9.0	15.0	24.0	53.0
Katmandu Follies	30.0	15.0	19.0	17.0	51.0	6.7	5.0	11.7	39.3
Pekinese Dream	18.0	9.0	9.9	15.0	33.9	8.0	10.0	18.0	15.9
Sheep Meadows	23.4	11.5	25.7	24.3	61.5	15.0	8.0	23.0	38.5
Wandering Wallabees	70.0	35.0	110.6	155.0	300.6	19.0	25.0	44.0	256.6
2001									
Flying Beetles	46.5	23.3	88.0	60.0	171.3	15.0	35.2	50.2	121.1
Real Pigs Have Feet	76.6	38.3	120.0	90.0	248.3	20.0	24.5	44.5	203.8
Shellie Memories	28.0	13.7	55.0	55.0	123.7	10.0	9.0	19.0	104.7
Spy Cats 3	22.0	11.0	66.0	46.0	123.0	8.0	10.0	18.0	105.0
Walter of Wisconsin: The Return	16.0	8.0	25.0	33.0	66.0	10.0	8.0	18.0	48.0

(a) Rentals equal distributor's share of U.S. box office.
(b) Domestic Other Revenue includes television, cable, video, and all other non-theatrical sources of revenue.
(c) Foreign Revenue includes both theatrical and ancillary revenues.
(d) Total Revenue equals Domestic Rentals, Domestic Other, and Foreign.
(e) Gross Profit before distributor's fee is removed.

© Copyright 2003 Crazed Consultant Films International

TABLE 10.4
CRAZED CONSULTANT FILMS INTERNATIONAL
**SELECTED FILMS WITH VARIED GENRES
U.S. BOX OFFICE AND BUDGETS ONLY
BUDGETS $8 TO $23 MILLION
YEARS 2002–2003**
(Millions of Dollars)

FILM	U.S. BOX OFFICE	BUDGET
Film 1	13.0	10.3
Film 2*	55.0	23.0
Film 3	48.0	20.0
Film 4**	150.0	18.0
Film 5	32.0	8.0
Film 6	33.8	15.0
Film 7	19.0	12.0
Film 8	57.2	11.0
Film 9*	23.4	11.0
Film 10	20.0	9.0
Film 11	16.5	12.0
Film 12	27.5	10.5

* Still in distribution as of [date of last report].
** Due to its extraordinary results, Film #4 is not included in the forecast.
Note: Domestic ancillary and all foreign data generally are not available until two years after a film's initial U.S. release.

Source: Business Strategies.

© Copyright 2003 Crazed Consultant Films International

TABLE 10.5
CRAZED CONSULTANT FILMS INTERNATIONAL
PROJECTED INCOME STATEMENT
(Millions of Dollars)

FILMS	BOX OFFICE	REVENUE DOMESTIC RENTALS	ANCILLARY	FOREIGN	TOTAL	COSTS BUDGET	P&A	TOTAL	DISTRIBUTOR'S GROSS PROFIT	EST. DIST. FEES	PRODUCER/ INVESTOR GROSS	COMPANY OVERHEAD	NET PRODUCER INVESTOR INCOME
Leonard's Love	3.0	1.5	3.5	3.5	8.5	0.5	3.5	4.0	4.5	3.0	1.5	0.3	1.2
Len's Big Thrill	10.0	5.0	18.0	11.0	34.0	2.5	8.8	11.3	22.7	11.9	10.8	0.5	10.3
Cat Follies	30.0	15.0	44.0	72.0	131.0	10.0	30.0	40.0	91.0	45.8	45.2	1.0	44.2
TOTAL	43.0	21.5	65.5	86.5	173.5	13.0	42.3	55.3	118.2	60.7	57.5	1.8	55.7

© Copyright 2003 Crazed Consultant Films International

TABLE 10.6
CRAZED CONSULTANT FILMS INTERNATIONAL
COMBINED CASH FLOW FOR THREE FILMS
(Millions of Dollars)

	YEAR 1				YEAR 2				YEAR 3				YEAR 4				YEAR 5				YEAR 6
	Qtr. 1	Qtr. 2	Qtr. 3	Qtr. 4	Qtr. 1	Qtr. 2	Qtr. 3	Qtr. 4	Qtr. 1	Qtr. 2	Qtr. 3	Qtr. 4	Qtr. 1	Qtr. 2	Qtr. 3	Qtr. 4	Qtr. 1	Qtr. 2	Qtr. 3	Qtr. 4	Qtr. 1
Leonard's Love																					
Production Budget	(0.1)	(0.2)	(0.1)	(0.1)																	
Prints and Ads							(1.8)	(0.5)	(0.9)	(0.3)											
Domestic Rentals							1.1	0.2	0.2												
Domestic Ancillary									1.8				1.7								
Foreign Revenue									1.0	0.9	0.5	0.8	0.3								
Distributor Fees									(1.5)				(1.5)								
Len's Big Thrill																					
Production Budget					(0.6)	(0.8)	(0.8)	(0.3)													
Prints and Ads											(4.7)	(1.1)	(2.2)	(0.8)							
Domestic Rentals											3.8	0.7	0.5								
Domestic Ancillary													9.0				9.0				
Foreign Revenue													3.2	2.6	1.7	2.6	0.9				
Distributor Fees													(6.0)				(5.9)				
Cat Follies																					
Production Budget									(2.5)	(3.0)	(3.0)	(1.5)									
Prints and Ads															(15.9)	(3.9)	(7.5)	(2.7)			
Domestic Rentals															11.2	2.3	1.5				
Domestic Ancillary																	22.0				22.0
Foreign Revenue																	20.9	17.3	10.8	17.3	5.7
Distributor Fees																	(20.3)				(25.5)
TOTALS	(0.1)	(0.2)	(0.1)	(0.1)	(0.6)	(0.8)	(1.5)	(0.6)	(1.9)	(2.4)	(3.4)	(1.1)	5.0	1.8	(3.0)	1.0	20.6	14.6	10.8	17.3	2.2
CUMULATIVE TOTAL	(0.1)	(0.3)	(0.4)	(0.5)	(1.1)	(1.9)	(3.4)	(4.0)	(5.9)	(8.3)	(11.7)	(12.8)	(7.8)	(6.0)	(9.0)	(8.0)	12.6	27.2	38.0	53.3	57.5

Note: Totals may not add due to rounding.

© Copyright 2003 Crazed Consultant Films International

Short Film Distribution

co-written with David Russell
President, Big Film Shorts

*"We now can move on to awakening the sleeping giant
that is short films."*

MARK LIPSY
Former executive vice president,
Miramax Films

A chapter on short film distribution? Does that mean you can write a business plan for short films? You may not be able to write a traditional business plan quite yet, but short films are the fastest growing and changing market segment in the entertainment industry; a sector of the industry that is changing faster than others. New revenue sources are developing rapidly. As a producer or director of short film, you need to know everything you can about the business side. We are both getting e-mails every day asking for information on finding funding for short films.

The whole industry knows about short films. To be more specific, the industry has always known about short films; they invented them. Prior to the last five or six years, student filmmakers were able to use short films as showcases; however, exhibitors and distributors didn't pay attention. Nor did the audience. Now that some exhibitors are daring to show their audiences short films, there is the emergence of a revenue-producing business.

This chapter can present only the tip of the iceberg. You may be reading it three years after publication. More than any other section of the book, you will have to do research to update the industry. There are minimal amounts of money for investing in short films now, but the future shows promise. This is only the beginning.

Two years ago, we contemplated writing a book about the business side of short films. It would have been very short, like the format itself. Why? There was not much to say; partly because the short form has never been fully exploited as a revenue source. People are just beginning to figure out how they can use short films beyond the usual filler. As money looms on the horizon for makers of short films, we feel we can now make this chapter worth your while.

WHAT IS A SHORT FILM?

There is nothing new about the format or the length. Compared to films today, silent films and talkies were short. The first public film screening by the Lumiere Brothers in 1895 included approximately ten short films lasting 20 minutes in total. The majority of their films were in actuality documentaries and some were comedies. In the first decade of the 20th century, Edison and others made one-reelers (the amount of film that would fit on one roll) that were ten to twelve minutes long. When projectors were modified to accommodate longer reels, a "short" became 20 minutes long. Newsreels each had been introduced in England in 1897 by the Frenchman Charles Pathé, but became popular in the 1920s. From the 1920s through 1940s, five companies—Fox Movietone, News of the Day, Paramount, RKO-Pathé, and Universal—made the five-minute long newsreels for the approximately 85 million people attending films each week. Along with the newsreels, the theaters also showed a variety of short films between 1919 and 1930; for example, Pathé produced a series of short documentaries for film audiences. In addition, Pete Smith and others made popular 15-minute black and white featurettes from the 1930s until the television revolution of the 1950s. The cartoons that were shown in addition to the newsreel and specialty shorts were usually five to eight minutes in length. At one point, a short film could actually run up to 59 minutes. As television delivered the news and feature films became longer, short subjects became unnecessary. At the moment, the most acceptable lengths at the more prestigious festivals range from 15 minutes for Cannes to a limit of 40 minutes long for Sundance, the Academy Awards, and Clermont-Farrand, the largest international short film market.

WHY MAKE A SHORT FILM?

Calling Card

A lot of people want to make a short film strictly as a calling card to introduce themselves to companies for future work or show to investors for their feature films. Filmmakers often think that a calling card film should be half an hour, in three acts, and an example of why someone should give you $3 million to make a feature. The experience of distributors is that you can't get anyone to watch a half-hour film. What will get their attention is a very successful five to 15-minute film that will get buzz like *George Lucas In Love* (eight minutes), *The Spirit of Christmas* (five minutes), or *Bottle Rocket* (11 minutes). The last film secured a studio deal for Wes Anderson and Owen Wilson, who went not only to a feature length version of their short but also to *Rushmore* and *The Royal Tenenbaums*, as well as individual projects.

More than one person has e-mailed Business Strategies saying that they had an investor with $500,000 to make a short film. Why would you want to do that? These days, with digital and the new technical readily equipment available, chances are you can make a full-length feature for the same amount of money. In that case, show that you can tell a story and make a feature. If not, make one or several short films for a lot less money.

Raise Money for a Feature

Making a short film that is essentially a promo for that $3 million feature is another useful purpose. The tendency often is to try to tell the entire story of the film. You want to give the potential investors a short glimpse of what the feature film is about. A short scene will do well, even a partial scene. If the film is intense, something very dramatic. If the film is a comedy, a short guffaw will do. You don't want to spend a lot of money. For one thing, you don't want the investor to think that you will be wasting his money. For another, you don't want to waste your own.

When making a short for this purpose, keep in mind that the film is essentially a piece of hype, the same way that a colorful brochure or a storyboard would be to entice the investor. The movie has the plus of showing some of the director's skill as well.

Filmmaking Experience

Making a short is the cheapest way to get the experience of going through the process. It is better to make mistakes on a $10,000 short than a $1 million feature. What filmmakers often don't realize is that the steps involved in making a five minute short are the same they will be using for the rest of their filmmaking lives. Many inexperienced people leave out steps in the beginning because they cut many corners, don't know what is essential or just plain forget important steps in their first effort. The result is that they end up with a film that is unreleasable or missing needed rights that prevent it ever being shown. One of our hardest tasks is to convince the filmmaker. Be smart and believe. TC Rice, Vice-President/ Distribution, Manhattan Pictures says,

> *"Shorts are essentially to the development of filmmakers, it is how they learn their craft. This is the whole process of learning by trial and error. No matter how many film courses anyone takes, they are no substitute for hands-on experience. Shorts are the training ground for the feature filmmakers of tomorrow."*

Make Money

Making money is another story. Most filmmakers don't start out to make a short film to sell. It never crosses their minds. Until now there have been few good reasons to think about it. The philosophy of the indie filmmaker was "just do it," just get something made. Well, that was in the good old days, the 1990s. Now there's potential for short films beyond making a calling card or getting experience. If you want to get some of your money back and sell or license your film in commercial markets, be aware of guild rules, distributors' requirements, music, and property rights. As more buyers eagerly anticipate short films, the differences between the short form and a long form are the variety of markets and the eventual amount of money the filmmaker is likely to make.

SOURCES OF FINANCING

Probably the most asked question for both of us is, "Where do I find the money?"Usually money for short films comes from two places: (1) family and friends, and (2) grants. Until more revenue sources open up, the money has to come from people who want to see your film made for either personal or business reasons and who don't expect a return on their investment. Until now, there has been no return to promise them. As we will see, this situation may be changing. At the moment, however, money invested in a short film should be considered a donation.

Family and Friends

If you want to raise money from a private investor, that person is usually a friend or member of your family. The only reason for someone to give you money for a short is to see their name on a screen, or because they love you. At the moment, it is unlikely an investor will make all their money back, much less a profit.

Grants

Getting a grant for a short film is not that different from getting one for a feature documentary. The big difference is that fewer foundations and companies are likely to be interested in shorts than features. Each grant has to be applied for with an understanding of what the granting body requires. The process can be very complicated. To write a successful grant application, you'll need to understand the granting philosophy of the donor organization and its budget.

One client, for example, applied for $30,000. Since the foundation had a $10,000 cap, the application was rejected. It would seem rational that they might award part of the budget; however, this foundation didn't work that way. As they only would fund one project a year, it was all or nothing.

Another short film client has submitted this story.

The biggest mistake I ever made in regard to trying to get a grant was in submitting what I thought at the time to be a flawless application and essay. Later I learned from the foundation's director that my mistake was not submitting any personal information about myself. I had, in effect, turned in a very professional, comprehensive, and worthy application but forgot that the people reviewing it wouldn't know anything about who I was as a person. Therefore, they felt no emotional connection to me whatsoever.

My advice is to be as forthright and transparent as possible so that the people reading your application will want to give you what you're asking for. In the case of grants, they need to not only like and admire your work but they like and admire you.

The grant market is so different from the commercial market that the filmmaker has to do extensive research on every organization to which she wants to apply. The Internet and the library have much reference material. In addition, when you approach a group ask as many questions as you can.

MARKETS

The market for short films has been very limited. While there are new markets opening up in theaters, television, cable and DVD, they are not yet mature. Nor do we know to what size they will grow. Still the filmmaker needs to understand how all the markets work in order to decide how to proceed. Carol Crowe of Apollo Cinema says,

> *The short film market continues to evolve. Apollo Cinema has quadrupled the number of cities where it tours the Oscar Shorts showcase theatrically in the U.S, which is a 300% increase over what we did just two years ago. Our sales to airlines and new media outlets also continue to grow. There are only four companies in the United States that distribute short films and each year we each continue to build and expand our businesses. We are all hopeful that the shorts will be more part of the mainstream and not on the outer edges of the art house arena.*

It takes a long time to sell short films, because there are not large companies, such as studios, taking them for worldwide distribution. Every sale is a one-on-one negotiation which has to be customized individually for the buyer. It is not unrealistic to have a film that will appeal to a majority of the world markets. Nevertheless, it takes as much, if not more, work than selling a feature film.

Festivals

Film festivals are a good way to get your film seen by a large number of people. There are several reasons to enter: have your film seen by potential buyers, create a name for yourself with feature film companies and investors, and make your film eligible for the

Academy Awards. Distributors, theatrical, television and cable buyers, critics, and other festival directors attend the major festivals and are always looking for interesting films. As with the festival discussion about features, the major competitive festivals give the filmmaker more chance for exposure. The competition for all these festivals is growing at an enormous rate. At the 2003 Sundance Film Festival, for example, there were 3,345 short film (compared to 2,100 the previous year) entries for 90 spots. However, being in any festival, whether competitive or not, may bring notice for your film.

Short Docs

Short documentaries are not accepted by all festivals. Cannes does not accept them in either the short film category or the Cinéfondation, which accepts short and medium-length films from schools. Sundance accepts short docs in its short film program, while there is a separate Oscar category for documentary short subjects. Which festivals do accept documentary shorts and in what category needs to be checked individually. Every day brings new opportunities. The Canadian Documentary Channel buys shorts as well as features. Sundance is starting a documentary channel, and recently, Japan established a new doc channel which accepts short films of 15 minutes and under. They license the films for two months as opposed to most buyers that want three years.

Worldwide

The markets for shorts are expanding at a more rapid pace than they have in the last 50 years. Bronwyn Kidd, Director Flickerfest Short Film Bureau (Australia), says,

> Short film is the truly independent storytelling medium of our generation, devoid of studio interference and film making by committee, it enables the individual to make some really unique insights into the moments, experiences and events that define our modern world. As interest in this independent art form continues to grow so too will the markets for short throughout the world.

Although there has always been a very small theatrical market worldwide for shorts, major theater chains in the U.S. are beginning to pay attention. At the moment, the U.S. has the only real theatrical market for shorts. Anything over six minutes generally gets knocked out of the theatrical ballpark, however. The broadcast markets want very short films also. Most buyers pay by the minute, so technically a company would have to pay more for half-hour films. For DVDs, the pay may not be by the minute, but it is a new market still finding its structure. TIVO is another. Currently, the company acquires shorts for a two-week exclusive, but does not pay anything for them. The filmmaker has to decide if the exposure (and possible loss of future sales) is worth it. Here is an example of a company realizing that there are new uses for the short film that people didn't see before.

In Europe and the other international markets, currently there is no theatrical distribution for shorts. Even in countries where the government supports the making of short films, the exhibitors choose not to comply with rules to show the films. On the other hand, those countries have a more lucrative ancillary market for shorts than the U.S. Jean Charles Mille, General Manager of Premium Films in France (one of the top three short film companies in Europe), says,

> *Our main objective is to motivate TV stations to broadcast shorts and our 140 international shorts from 17 countries is our best asset. The TV and the DVD rights are the sole important revenue for short films producers and the good news is that more and more European TV channels are interested in airing shorts not only as fillers but also in some special short programs and they don't hesitate to broadcast them on prime-time! We are confident in short films in Europe and hope that the digital broadcasting will increase the sales.*

Advertainments/Advertorials

Questions keep coming to us about short films as advertisements or "advertorials." There are two types going on at the moment. Most filmmakers are aware that BMW and a few other companies have commissioned filmmakers to do short films. These films, often referred to as "advertainment" are product promotions disguised as entertaining short films. At the moment, these shorts are commissioned by the company which hires well-known directors, such as Ang Lee and Guy Ritchie.

Another new concept, "advertorials," is from Regal CineMedia Corp. In October 2002, they announced an agreement with NBC followed by one with Turner in January 2003 to produce "entertainment snippets" to be part of Regal's 20-minute preshows in their theaters. Two other agreements were expected but had not been announced when this book went to press. These films are not the same program in which Regal plans to show short films from indies with specific features on their Cinema Arts Screens.

The Internet

As the market works today, putting a short film on the Internet is a deal breaker for any possibility of selling the film through other media. Distributors insist on having the Internet rights, because the buyers want them. It doesn't matter whether the buyers have any plans to use the Internet rights. Even if they don't use them, they don't want anyone else to. If HBO just paid $16,500 for a film, they don't want to see it pop up on the Internet.

The big channels are still going to want exclusives, because the Internet is worldwide. For example, HBO may buy the film for the U.S. but insist on a worldwide exclusive for the Internet rights. If the Internet could be split, then the cable channel would probably only want the U.S. rights. That territory is their only concern. Since the other channels don't pay as much, they either don't ask for the Internet to be included or, if they do, don't ask for an exclusive. Since the distributor doesn't know in advance what the deal will be, Internet rights have to be available.

If HBO has the worldwide rights, and there is a television or cable buyer in another country for the film, the distributor can negotiate. For example, HBO has the rights for a short for distribution in the U.S., including the Internet rights. Then a month later, Canal Plus wants it for Canal Plus International, which covers a lot of Europe. It is likely that the sale can be done. Canal Plus will discount for the fact that those rights are currently held. If the distributor says that HBO has the rights for the world but has no plans to use them at the moment, the European company might ask how long the contract is. HBO is not going to relicence it, nor does the European company care. The goal of both companies is to keep the film off the Internet. Sometimes they even pay extra for that right. When the HBO contract runs out, it can be licensed to the European company.

Another example is when a distributor has a film for which an American company has nonexclusive rights. There is a buyer in

Japan, who wants exclusive Internet rights. It can be worked out with the Japanese company by offering them the exclusive for their country, and an agreement that it will not relicence the short to any competitors in Japan who are going to subtitle it in Japanese. That is all they are really concerned about. They know that worldwide is worldwide; however, an American company is not going to subtitle the film in Japanese. If the distributor has nonexclusive deals like that, he can make that deal in every country but each of these contracts has to be negotiated separately with each buyer.

The Internet is not a market now. However, it could become a valuable market, when there is really some kind of convergence and Internet companies will pay for the privilege. Since most of the films that short film distributors see are unsaleable, showcasing on the Internet is a way to go. If it is only a calling card and you have no intention of ever trying to make any money from the film, go ahead. Read all contracts carefully, however, all the way to the end. All the Internet sites that feature short films need content, which works in the filmmaker's favor. Before signing anything, take the contract to your attorney as you would with a feature film.

POTENTIAL REVENUE

If you are making a 10-minute film, the likely return is $5,000. Big Film Shorts uses the formula of $15 to $100 a minute with a film selling to five different markets on average. Don't interpret this to mean the longer the film, the more money. Ten minutes and under is still the best. The longer a film, the less saleable it is, and the less likely the revenue formula is to be pertinent. As mentioned above it takes a long time to sell short films, because every sale is one-on-one. But it is realistic that, if you have a film that appeals to most of the world markets, you can make back $5,000; in some cases, you can even make more.

Big Film Shorts has had the experience of selling seven-minute films to HBO (two years exclusive on any channel HBO owns) for $16,500 for just the U.S. market. Don't get carried away with the amount. HBO buys very few short films and not all at that price. Such films usually show on Cinemax as fillers and interstitials after features. Meaning "in between," interstitials are usually 20 to 130 seconds long and were developed as a form of entertaining advertising for television. The term has evolved to be anything that fits in the space that might otherwise be dead air. The same deal can work with Showtime. Whatever price Showtime pays entitles the company to show your film on its other channels: MTV, Comedy Channel, and the Sundance Channel.

Quality of Product

With short films, as with a feature, how the movie needs to look depends on what you are going to do with it. For theatrical release, the product has to look crisp and clear whether it is on digital or 35 mm. Filmmakers often tend to think that they can make grainy pictures. But if you are going into the marketplace, it is imperative to be on film and look like it is film; no matter what genre. In general the buyers and the audience do demand the same production quality. The movie has to compete in every way with the other content in a given market. Content is paramount, if it passes all the other criteria. A slick looking film with no content only seems to work if a Hollywood studio made it, long or short.

Unless a short film is going to have a theatrical life there will be no need for a 35 mm print. But all the other formats that will be delivered to the various worldwide markets will look a whole better if they all come from a 35 mm shoot.

Distributors say that most films don't sell, because most films are not good. It's all the ingredients coming together and making magic. Quality is the end result. If it's saleable, it's watchable; if it's watchable, it's because good talent made it. That doesn't mean the whole world will love it, but there's an audience out there for it somewhere.

Docs can get away with digital and CGI animation of anything else created on computers. The audience doesn't demand the same quality as they do with fiction films. They want docs to look more like the creator meant them to look. With a narrative, however, the audience wants it to look like a clean print.

Unfortunately, markets vary. Big Film Shorts has a film that is being delivered to HBO that was shot on HD in 16:9 (the digital wide screen format) and transferred to 35 mm for festivals. Now it is in a theatrical exhibition program with Regal Entertainment. HBO will not accept the 1.85:1 ratio that all the prints and tapes were made with, as they require full frame television ratio (1.33:1). On the other hand, major European broadcasters have been transmitting wide screen in Pal Plus (analog) and now in digital broadcasting.

There isn't any reason it can't work both ways. There are several conversion systems available. Check which is the best way to go, before making your film. Generally, no matter what system you edit on, distributors in the short film business prefer films that have been shot on 35 mm.

Even more important then the look is the sound. The reality of the marketplace is that the short has to compete with the highest-end feature in terms of sound. Whether on a theater screen or on cable, the film is going to be paired with a feature. It has to fit in the same class of filmmaking as the feature. For example, Big Film Shorts had the experience of having a film that was monosound. Everyone in the theater had just heard the last booming trailer. This little short came on with monosound, and the audience started complaining, thinking that there was something wrong with the theater's sound system. The exhibitor stopped showing the short.

CONTRACTS

Owning Your Film

In order to "own" the copyright, the filmmaker must have releases (signed permission) or contracts for everything in the picture, as he would have to have for a feature film. This list may include:

- Actors and extras. Any non-union actor and even regular people like friends and relatives must sign a release giving you permission to use their likeness and voice in all possible exhibition venues. It is not necessary to get every person on a street or in a crowd to sign a release as long as the camera does not linger on them and is a doing a "drive-by."
- Sound: music, effects. The use of music without permission is the single most abused element in short film production. The producer must get permission from both the owners of the publishing and the sync rights.
- Locations: any private property, public property (usually via permits). You also need releases that give you permission to use someone's private property for filming, their car, building, a sign, their pond or their woods. In other words, if it's not your property, it's theirs. In the case of public property, you need a permit from the local

authorities (see your film commission). For drive-by shots, be careful not to "establish" a building, or even a FedEx van, or that 18-wheeler with the famous brand name logo on the side. If the camera lingers too long, it could be inferred that you are incorporating that object into your story line. Legal complications show up, when you least expect them!

- Décor: Any and everything on the walls or furniture or exteriors of buildings and other people's copyrights: posters, paintings, book covers, etc. Just when you thought you were safe by shooting in your own apartment, hold on. Look around. An object may be in your house, but is it really yours? Louise has Indian paintings on her wall. However, when a commercial was being filmed in her home, the Indian paintings on her wall were removed. Why? Case law has established that a reproduction for sale could not be made of any of the paintings without the artists' permission. If one of the paintings was a permanent background in the shot, it could be construed that the painting was being used for a commercial purpose. Why tempt the litigation gods?
- Clips: stock, excerpts from other works. The producer must get releases for everything seen or heard in the movie. Borrowing a nice scene from your videotape collection is not allowed.

What do you do? Spend all your time getting signatures? It is better to be safe than sorry. In *Clearance & Copyright*, Michael Donaldson says that it is always safest to clear. "Fair use" is mentioned in the copyright law; however, "the law doesn't give a list of uses that are always and under all circumstances permitted under the doctrine of fair use."

Deliverables

Any distributor of short films will require roughly the same delivery of materials (at your expense) as a feature film distributor. These items may include:

- one BETA SP (stereo) videotape master of the picture in the NTSC format (also in PAL format if requested)

- 5 VHS NTSC videotape copies
- one 3/4" dub from the videotape master, if requested
- post-production script
- music cue sheet
- copyright registration for the film and other chain-of-title and insurance information
- key artwork
- stills (usually color) in JPEG format
- release print(s) in available format if requested for theatrical rental(s)
- current list of festivals and awards
- an authorization to the laboratories and suppliers of, respectively, pre-print materials and foreign tracks and accessories to accept our orders for materials to permit distributor to service agreements
- copies of all paperwork giving permission and release for use of actors or statement regarding SAG agreement, writers, music, trademarks, and logos; clips or excerpts from other copyrighted material, and locations

Guilds

The Screen Actors Guild (SAG) offers a variety of contracts which allow a filmmaker to "employ" professional, card-carrying union actors. There are contracts that allow only screening at festivals. Sounds good? What if someone comes along and wants to sell the film to television or show it to a paying audience? You must renegotiate the contract with SAG and the actors. The Student and Experimental contracts cannot be converted for revenue-producing markets without each actor's permission. This puts the actor in a bargaining position in terms of money and other demands. In addition, according to the experience of short film producers, SAG does not allow the filmmaker to pre-negotiate a "what if" with the actors. From the Guild's point of view, it is protecting the actor from being taken advantage of, because he was willing to be in your 10-minute film. On the other hand, the actors can demand more money than the film will ever make. This happened to one of our filmmakers under the experimental contract. Not expecting the short film to be distributed, he paid his actors because "it was the right thing to do." When the opportunity for distribution arose, he had to get the actors' permission and pay them a second time. Of course, one of the actors then held out for a big payday.

If you have any thoughts of going to a festival, market, or finding distribution in any other way, it is best to go with the low-budget or, perhaps, modified budget contract. Before deciding, check the current contract information on SAG's indie site (www.sagindie.com), find the location of the nearest office, and meet with a representative to discuss all the possible scenarios for your film. There is also a handy "Film Contracts Digest" that SAG can send you. Consider the optimum possibilities for the film and ask the representative what the next step will be, and the next, and the next, etc. Do not assume, as many feature filmmakers do, that SAG won't know. They are very good at knowing if anyone owes their members money.

The Directors' Guild (DGA) also has an experimental contract. It is applicable, if the purpose of the film is to provide a DGA member with experience or to serve as a "resume piece." The film may be entered in festivals and submitted for award consideration to the Academy of Motion Picture Arts and Sciences (Oscars) and/or the Academy of Television Arts and Sciences Awards (Emmys). It cannot be intended for commercial release in any medium, which includes theaters, videocassettes, free television, public television, pay television, cable or the Internet and any other commercial source that may come along. Note that this severely limits your distribution options. In addition, the total budget for the film has to be no more than $50,000 and the running time of the project, as edited, no more than 30 minutes. Again, check with the contracts on the DGA's website and speak with your nearest representative. If you have any thought of commercial uses for the film, it may be best to follow their low-budget contract.

THE FUTURE

Worldwide markets at least doubled from 1996 to 2002. Looking at the markets that are starting to exist now, the commercial opportunity for short films will double again in the next two years. This estimate should be considered conservative. Undoubtedly, the buyers that are coming on board now will prompt other companies to copy them. When people see that there is money to be made with short films, they will find new ways to create more demand.

Big film shorts, while exploring the opportunity for more theatrical screening of short films in the United States, recently made agreements for the viewing of shorts via Video-On-Demand (VOD).

This market has just begun to open and promises to be a profitable opportunity for film makers. On different systems—such as, Rogers Cable, Cox, Time-Warner, and Comcast—they are using different system labels, but it is all VOD. There are two kinds of VOD: pay-per-view and free-for-view. In the future, the goal is to get sponsors for the free-for-view showings. Although some of the cable systems have technical problems with VOD, the problems should be fixed in the next couple of years.

Movieola in Canada has had the first 24-hour short film channel in North America running over a year with 500,000 subscribers currently. AtomTV is another planned channel. In addition, new specialty cable channels are planned to feature genres such as docs, gay and Lesbian, extreme sports, whatever. Canal Plus even has a separate division that buys short films to sell specifically to countries on the continent of Africa. This type of proliferation is important, because the fee a buyer like Canal Plus pays is based on the number of territories they buy for.

From our perspective, the future for shorts is bright. Since everything is new, we can't give the short film market a dollar value. However, as companies see others making money from short films, we believe that they will rush to jump on the bandwagon. New uses are evolving every day. The number of buyers are increasing, as are the audiences to which the films are available. As people become used to seeing short films, it is hoped there will be a larger market for video and DVD collections.

INDEX